I Was a Communist for the FBI: Matt Cvetic

The true life and times of undercover agent Matt Cvetic

by

R.E. "Gus" Payne

authorHOUSE™

1663 LIBERTY DRIVE, SUITE 200
BLOOMINGTON, INDIANA 47403
(800) 839-8640
WWW.AUTHORHOUSE.COM

First published by AuthorHouse 08/31/04

ISBN: 1-4184-8843-7 (sc)

Printed in the United States of America
Bloomington, Indiana

This book is printed on acid-free paper.

DEDICATION

To the memory of Matt Cvetic and his family, for all they endured for their love of country.

Special thanks to Sara Williams for the patience of reading and re-reading the manuscrpt as editorial assistant and C.W. at the Pittsburgh Post-Gazette for his assistance.

TABLE OF CONTENTS

INTRODUCTION

Uncovering a tangled web of officially orchestrated deception is never easy. We can only hope that we did well in unraveling the true story of the life of Pittsburgh's Matt Cvetic, who served as an undercover agent for the FBI in the Communist Party for nine years, 1941 to 1950. Cvetic is a rather forgotten and misunderstood story from the tumultuous years of "McCarthyism".

This narrative is true, as far as we can know. We shall never be confident of all of the facts of Cvetic's life because the very nature of what he did was clandestine. Even after becoming a public figure in 1950, we do not know he told us everything he knew about the Communist Party or even about the FBI, for that matter. But there is ample proof that the FBI, especially in Pittsburgh, honored and appreciated Cvetic, as on every opportunity given, they reported their confidence to FBI Director J. Edgar Hoover.

It is not our intention here to eulogize Cvetic but, simply, to give him recognition for what he did. What he did was courageous and perilous. For nine years, he lived under extreme pressure, at all times in fear of being discovered as a mole. During this period, he did forsake his family and he and they suffered ridicule and pain. His sacrifices were enormous.

Matt Cvetic was a great and fearless man at a time when America needed a great and fearless man.

R E. Payne

www.repayne.com

New Orleans

July 2004.

1

THE BACKGROUND

"With the tiniest Communist Party in the world, the United States was behaving as though on the verge of bloody revolution," wrote Arthur Miller (Timebends, p. 311). In *Film and Politics in America*, 42 anti-Communist films are listed as being produced in the years 1951-53 (p. 187). One of these films is the movie; *I Was A Communist For The FBI.* Produced by Warner Brothers, the movie is semi-based on the exploits of an undercover agent for the FBI, Matt Cvetic. It is about a man who "single-handedly" knocked the Communist Party to its knees in western Pennsylvania. Although it is clearly not a documentary, the movie was nominated for an Academy Award as the best documentary for the year 1951.

This book chronicles the life and times of Matt Cvetic. It is written to put into perspective 1) the contributions made to raising the specter of communism to the near hysterical level it reached during the late 1940's and the 1950's, 2) Cvetic's testimony before the House Un-American Activities Committee (UHAC), and 3) the true jeopardy in which he placed his own life for the sake of our country and the FBI. Cvetic served undercover as the FBI's agent for an incredible nine years, 1941 to 1950.

FBI Director J. Edgar Hoover had enormous success in discovering and exposing communism and its ideologies. He led the nation's law enforcement communities into a prolonged fight against radicalism. At no time during his tenure did he cease to hold the view that it was mandatory to root out the communists in order to expose their political aspirations and subversive activities.

Anti-Communism grew substantially as a result of the labor struggles of the 1930's. The presence of communists in unions shaped a legitimate reason for its enemies to organize and persuade the government to battle against communism. This resulted in the creation of the House Un-American Activities Committee (HUAC) in 1938. Senator Joseph McCarthy's Permanent Investigating Subcommittee of the Government Operations Committee became prominent in the 1950's, however even today, many mistakenly associate McCarthy with HUAC, this even though McCarthy was in the U.S. Senate and not the U.S. House of Representatives.

Many on the staff of HUAC were former FBI agents. The committee was not a destination of choice for most members of Congress, in all probability because much of the publicity caused by HUAC in its early days created the impression that the committee often shot from the hip, unable to support many of the accusations being made public by its all too-eager staff. However, despite its shortcomings, the committee's power grew as it became more skillful at its investigations and curtailed its ridiculous name-calling.

The Truman Administration's Attorney General, J. Howard McGrath, was a passionate anti-communist. He referred to communists as "pagans" who sought to "enslave mankind." He was particularly anxious about the socialist/communist ideology gaining ground on college and university campuses, hence, he urged educators to invite anti-communists speakers to address the students during class and/or general assemblies. He warned that college professors themselves might also be communist, and many have the chance to chip away at the principles of American justice and liberty by advocating the ideology of the Soviet Union.

With the rising public support against communism, along with the disposition and backing of the Truman Administration in line with Director Hoover's anti-communism law enforcement views, it becomes easy to understand why the HUAC and McCarthy had such success in further reaching out their investigations of communism in various arenas: the movies, work places and in social and other organizations.

Even though inactive during the years of WW II, the HUAC capitalized on the public's fascination with Hollywood celebrities by calling them to testify. Under the chairmanship of J. Parnell Thomas of New Jersey, an investigation was called to establish the influence of Communists in the movie industry, and to discern whether their propaganda was spread through the movies.

There were legitimate grounds to believe that the communists hoped to use motion pictures for propaganda purposes. The Soviets encouraged it. Here is what Joseph Stalin said on the subject: "The cinema is not only a vital agitprop device for the education and political indoctrination of the workers, but is also a fluent channel through which to reach the minds and shape the desires of people everywhere...The task is to take this affair into your hands, and vigorously execute it in every field"(Citizen News, 1951). There is more than enough evidence to suggest that the party attempted to gain control of the talent and craft unions, and that Hollywood was a major target of the American Communist Party.

To exemplify how important the HUAC 'red' hearings were in Hollywood, consider the about face made by actor John Garfield. In October 1947 he released a statement issued by the Hollywood Branch of the Committee for the First Amendment. The statement declared reservation that he and the others signing the statement considered the hearings "…morally wrong because any investigation into political beliefs of the individual is contrary to the basic principles of democracy. Any attempt to curb freedom of expression and to set arbitrary standards of Americanism is in itself disloyal to both the spirit and the letter of our Constitution." In 1950, Garfield was summoned to appear before the committee. "I have always hated communism. It is a tyranny which threatens our country and the peace of the world. Of course, then, I have never been a member of the Communist Party, or a sympathizer with any of its doctrines. I will be pleased to cooperate with the committee." Obviously, when under duress, Garfield took the path of least resistance. He was not alone.

Numerous cooperating witnesses at the HUAC hearings on the Communist Infiltration of Hollywood Motion Picture Industry were influential and they helped reap publicity for the committee. They were: Ronald Reagan (chief of the Screen Actors Guild), Louis B. Mayer (a studio head), Jack Warner (also a studio boss), actor Robert Montgomery, Walt Disney, Adolph Menjou, Robert Taylor and Gary Cooper.

The committee called a total of 41 witnesses, pronouncing nineteen as communists or sympathizers. The official declaration was that the 19 were "unfriendly", a qualification earned by them because they refused to answer questions about their political beliefs in open committee. The list was further wiggled down to what has become known as "The Hollywood Ten." They were: director, Edward Dmytryk and nine screenwriters, Alyah Bessie, Herbert Biberman, Lester Cole, Ring Lardner, Jr., John Howard Lawson, Albert Maltz, Samuel Omintz, Adrian Scott and Dalton Trumbo.

In all fairness, these ten individuals had unquestioned rights to avoid self-incrimination, a guarantee of the 5th Amendment and they also had the guarantees of the 1st Amendment of freedom of speech and association. Opponents of the committee were justified in pointing out that those serving on the committee were acting as judge and jury. The so-called "Hollywood

Ten" were mostly guilty of refusing to incriminate themselves, and of refusing to help the committee find them 'guilty.' Spinning these hearings into trials did not help with public opinion.

On November 24, 1947 following the HUAC hearing, Hollywood's major studio bosses and other executives issued a statement: "We will not knowingly employ a Communist or a member of any party or group which advocates the overthrow of the Government of the United States by force, or by any illegal or unconstitutional method." The Hollywood Ten were fired and ineligible for rehire unless the committee cleared them of suspicion. All ten were charged with contempt of Congress, each serving six to 12 months, except for Dmytryk, who was released early for later cooperating with the committee.

Another series of hearings was held in Washington and in Hollywood in 1951, under John S. Wood, the director of HUAC. A list of more than 300 motion picture employees was produced, all of whom were allegedly then communists or had been communists, and/or were members of the Communist Party. About 200 of the persons on the list were at work when the list was published. They all were fired. All the names were added to a 'blacklist' of persons who were no longer eligible for work in the industry.

———

To a huge extent, Matt Cvetic has gotten a bum rap from some writers, particularly Daniel J. Leab, who penned *"I Was a Communist for the FBI"* (Pennsylvania State University, 2000), a book supposedly entirely about Cvetic and his life. Leab makes much of the fact that Cvetic was not an FBI "special agent," assigned to infiltrate the western Pennsylvania Communist Party in Pittsburgh. Leab likes to point out that the Bureau clarified its responses to inquiries by stating very directly that Cvetic "was not a Special Agent of the FBI." In fact, there is a very minor difference between being "an agent of the FBI" and a "special agent" who is assigned undercover duties. The simple fact is that the FBI persuaded civilian Cvetic to join the party, infiltrate it and deliver all the information he gathered about their activities to the local FBI office in Pittsburgh. For doing this, he was paid by the FBI, at least during the last seven years. He filed thousands of pages of reports with the Bureau over the nine years he was undercover.

Chosen by the FBI office in Pittsburg with Hoover's personal approval, Cvetic was at the time of his recruitment a relatively low-level federal employee in the United States Employment Service in Pittsburgh. Writers with a left-leaning inclination often paint Cvetic as a drunk, undependable adult, who was irresponsible in his personal life and unproductive on the job. How can this be? It is certainly safe to assume that the FBI thoroughly checked out Cvetic before recruiting him, having run exhaustive background checks on his professional and personal life.

When asked to join the party as an informant for the FBI, Cvetic was told that he would have to give up his life as he knew it, to "walk, talk, and eat Communism. In other words, be a Red for all intent and purposes." (The Big Decision, Cvetic, 1959). He infiltrated the party, pleasing the party leaders by helping communists get hired at the federal employment service where he worked, and became active in national issues concerning the Slavic communities in Pittsburg, Chicago, Cleveland and other cities. Being from Slavic descent, and having knowledge of the languages, he rose to Executive Secretary of the American Slav Congress (ASC), a leftist group that alleged to represent millions of Americans of Slav descent.

Cvetic served with fervor. He earned the respect and admiration of the Pittsburgh office of the Bureau where FBI agents valued the depth of his weekly written reports, some of which were 50 pages or more. Because of Cvetic, the FBI was able to wire up meeting rooms where high level meetings were held by the communists. Cvetic's upward movement in the party was slow, meticulous, and agonizing. Cvetic, as an undercover agent became a kaleidoscopic personality, changing as he had to, in order to placate his comrades. Cvetic was most helpful on following the plans and activities of western Pennsylvania communists who were working in Slavic languages. Cvetic spoke Slovenian, Croatian, Serbian, Lithuanian, Russian, Slovak and Polish. Cvetic even helped to produce radio shows in these languages and was the most reliable eye on this target group that the FBI had. Hoover himself appreciated Cvetic's efforts, confirming that he thought Cvetic was the best chance the agency had of penetrating the inner sanctum of the Communist Party. (*I Was a Communist for the FBI*, Leab).

The truth is that no matter how often or how many writers find fault with Cvetic, he was by the strictest standards applied, an extremely valuable undercover agent for the FBI. He endured nine torturous years during which he never had a minute of peace or total confidence that he would not be discovered as a mole and killed by angry comrades. Despite how

Cvetic came out from undercover, and the FBI's dissatisfaction with his method, Cvetic remained "one of the most productive informants" the FBI ever had. To do what he was asked by the FBI and the CP, Cvetic needed intellect without morals, ability without scruple and above all, courage without honor.

What were the secrets of Cvetic's survival? We cannot answer with absolute certainty because much of what we see is clouded in contradiction. Who is to say how much of what Cvetic testified at HUAC is true? Was it diluted or edited by the FBI? These are things we do not know.

Edward Dmytryk, the director and member of The Hollywood Ten, testified before UHAC, April 25, 1951. In regard to Cvetic, here is what he told the UHAC: "I would like to read a wire I got. The important part of this wire is simply that it relates an interview on last Sunday night between Louella Parsons and a man named Matt Cvetic. I believe he is the man who wrote a book called "I Was a Communist for the FBI." Louella Parsons asked him, "What about the argument that these trials drive the Reds further underground?" He replied, "Don't fall for that. The Reds try to put that idea across to discourage these trials, but the truth is the Commies always work underground. Anything that brings them in the open hurts them." He was then asked about the cleverness of the communists at recruiting top candidates for membership, Cvetic replied, "The really frightening cleverness of the Communists is how they understand appealing to people's best emotions-their tolerance-their broadmindedness, and then use those good emotions for their own end."

The volume of evidence available for research clearly reveals that Cvetic was a consummate undercover agent who worked under great pressure and delivered the information needed by the FBI. When Cvetic surfaced he gave out over 300 names and contacts he made while undercover for the FBI. It is not fair to criticize him for this or to dismiss him as a "paid witness", since he was acting under the prevailing belief that the Communist Party was an organized criminal or subversive organization, and that what he was doing is what crime fighters do.

Perhaps as some authors have declared, Cvetic's love of glory was excessive, however he was entitled to a certain amount of this following nine years without any public recognition. Cvetic was a man of intelligence, courage, and integrity, but he was not perfect. For his time and place, for what he was asked to do, he was outstanding.

Cvetic was what he had to be to do what he had to do. Time and prejudice have no doubt destroyed some of his story. Emergencies make men and it is undeniable that the jeopardy he was in as an undercover agent was real. He had to be strong to keep his faults from defeating his purposes. He was a man full of human contradictions. Perhaps his mind was not as good as his press releases but he had his share of qualities that helped him survive the nine years while undercover.

Cvetic could be cruel and kind, violent and gentle, petty, generous, cheap, cunning, naïve, crude, candid, and frankly, dishonest. He learned to maneuver. Yes, he was driven by ambition and ego but if he had not been, would he have survived? He had an appetite for intrigue. He learned to live a life of lies. Truthfully, self-preservation was the active essence of his motives.

The legal counsel for UHAC, Frank S. Tavenner, Jr., in opening remarks at one session, referred to Cvetic in his opening remarks. This is what he said: "I need only remind you that the testimony of Matthew Cvetic virtually destroyed, for the time being at least, the power and influence of the Communist Party in western Pennsylvania. "

Western Pennsylvania was a hotbed of Communist Party activity and was the primary focal point in the United States for the recruitment of diverse ethnic groups. In addition to disclosure of activity on the Slavic communities, Cvetic, in his first appearance in public after breaking his cover, told UHAC that Steve Nelson was the district organizer whose responsibility included significant "Negro work". Cvetic's appearance in 1950 at UHAC rocked the anti-communism groups and spurred public opinion. His description of the inner workings of the party and how it was structured confirmed the necessity of having undercover agents follow the planning of this subversive organization. Steve Nelson is also an important part of this story.

Nelson, the un-welcomed focus of Cvetic's public debut, was well-loved by radicals. He had a long history as a dedicated leftist. Nelson had been under suspicion by the FBI for years and was even suspected of being involved in atomic espionage through his association with a woman who later married J. Robert Oppenheimer (Cold War at Home, Philip Jenkins). The Pittsburgh media was unrelenting in tagging Nelson as an alleged "atomic spy". One story went so far as to say that Nelson had given orders to many in the area as to how to act when and if a war between the United States and Soviet Union erupted.

Nelson's efforts secured solid footholds for Communists in the ethnic communities and in certain other organizations and, of course, the unions in the Pittsburgh area. Everything was on cruise control for Nelson and the CP in Pittsburg when Cvetic went public in 1950 before the congressional committee to expose the local party members and their activities. As a result of Cvetic's revelations, an organized and publicly orchestrated hunt for Communists took place under the headlines of the Pittsburgh press. A local judge, Michael Musmanno, seized the moment (and the headlines) by proclaiming that every single Communist in the area would be rooted out and persecuted. A few weeks following Cvetic's testimony, Musmanno, some police and Cvetic, raided the regional Communist Party headquarters. Nelson was arrested and tried with two other party members for sedition (calling for the overthrow of capitalism).

The case took more than two years to wind itself through the justice system. During trial proceedings, Cvetic's exploits as an undercover agent were hitting the big screen in "I Was a Communist for the FBI." The worldwide premiere of the movie was in Pittsburg and the mayor proclaimed "Matt Cvetic Day" to be celebrated with a parade. As if the publicity generated by the movie was not enough, Nelson had to defend himself as he was without attorneys for most of the trial. Nelson was convicted but the conviction was later overturned. Musmanno parlayed his newfound notoriety and celebrity into a judgeship on the state Supreme Court, but he failed to secure the Democratic nomination for the U.S. Senate in 1964.

Another development spawned by Cvetic and the notoriety resulting from his undercover revelations was that the Communist Party in Pennsylvania became the object of an open war against the communists. Those ethnic organizations and unions where Communist had made considerable gains since the 1930's, at one time having an estimated membership of 10,000 or more, became notable targets. Communists had some clout in the Westinghouse plant as well as in the unions. Congressional and other hearings descended upon Pennsylvania to capitalize on the public support generated by Cvetic. State legislators passed new, tough laws, one outlawing the Communist Party and another requiring loyalty oaths from state employees. Matt Cvetic took credit for much of this and it is difficult to argue that anyone else had more influence on the psyche of the public at the time.

Too many writers view this period as one of repression and suppression of rights. That is one side of the story. It can be argued that law enforcement, Congress and even state legislators overreacted to the threat of communism by creating too many laws and giving law enforcement too many powers. Certainly the term used for this period, "McCarthyism", has come to mean one senator acting as prosecutor, judge and jury. Unfortunately, it also obscures the truth of the other side of the story, the one told by Cvetic. The question to be asked is this: Why did his testimony in Pittsburgh in 1950 kick off a wave of support from the public to seek out and stamp out communism?

The answer is that there was enough truth in what he revealed to scare the average law abiding, patriotic citizen into demanding action. Individual rights were at stake but so were national security and the survival of institutions in government. The public demanded that these rights and institutions be defended, and that the nation confront the hard questions that needed to be answered for state security.

Many editorialists of the period had conflicting views. Some warned that in the end, protecting the security of the nation, although vital, must not be accomplished at the cost of limiting freedoms or human rights. Many Americans had doubts about just how serious the threat of communism was: however, the majority wanted the problems relating to communism and national security solved without the undoing of liberties.

There was little public support for widespread law enforcement to arrest and prosecute Communists for "thought crimes". What Cvetic did was to describe the structure and organization not of a political party, but of a group of subversives threatening the very liberties everyone cherished. When he told how the party leaders in Pittsburgh drank champagne and joked about how great they would have it when the Communist Party took charge in America, the average person got the message. These communists were not all do-gooders desiring to heal racial inequalities or economic deprivation, or who wanted to change the world for the better. They were opportunists, misfits and profiteers who had to conceal their true aspirations from the public.

Cvetic's life had been tortuous for nine years. Every time the doorbell rang or whenever he was suddenly called to meetings, he wondered, was this the day he was discovered as a mole? Was this a family member calling again to plead for him to leave the CP before his mother died? He never knew when his tenure as an undercover agent would end. Finally, he decided to end it himself. Leab claims he was fired but this again could have been part of an overall FBI plot to stir the public's attention.

———

Although short (5'5") and pudgy, Cvetic made a good first impression. Despite his small stature he derived a commanding presence from his keen eyes and sharp grooming. He had the confidence of a salesman, which he was from time to time during his spotted career before going to work for the FBI. Matt was the proud son of immigrant parents who had managed to find a good life in the Pittsburgh area. He had six brothers and four sisters. He married Marie Barsh on August 15, 1931. They had twin sons, Matt Jr. and Richard. Matt and Marie divorced in 1946. He had a reputation for liking women.

Cvetic attended Roman Catholic schools but probably did not graduate from high school. He did claim to have completed many correspondence courses, mostly in the law enforcement profession. He began his work at what became the U.S. Employment Service in Pittsburgh in 1937. Circumstances alter careers and this is certainly what happened in Cvetic's life. He was recruited by the FBI in 1941 and thus his life changed forever. Unfortunately, in the end, he left behind little more than creditors.

It is interesting to speculate what exactly were the character qualities and flaws that interested the FBI in Cvetic. His recruitment was aggressive. It took Cvetic two years to gain the confidence of the CP in Pittsburgh to finally gain membership. He then progressed from an unpaid FBI informant to a paid one.

While it is obvious now that Cvetic was certainly capable of using deception, intimidation, intrigue, ingratitude, perjury, treachery, and other tools, it is not clear at all how the FBI decided on Cvetic or knew he had these abilities. He was ideal for the role he was to play. He became a man of instinct and not thought. His unquestioning self-confidence carried him through many tough spots.

Cvetic's appearances beginning in 1950 at UHAC and court hearings were mixed. His critics blame him for vacillating on almost everything, and all too often, remaining on the surface of things. He was seen too often only as an exhibitionist who waved his ego in public. But how will we ever know how much of this was at the instruction of the FBI? We won't ever know for sure. His moments in the sun were brief and illusory.

The purpose of the hearings was to identify current or former members of the Communist Party. Usually it was an ex-communist who appeared before the committee and named names or suggested they knew whether others were Communists or not. When the committee received a list of names using this method, these individuals were called upon and were interrogated about their communist affiliation. It was a very simple process. Again, depending upon how cooperative the witnesses, another list would usually result. And so on.

Of course, some witnesses refused to answer the questions by asserting their 1st Amendment or 5th Amendment rights. Witnesses in this category knew they could be charged with contempt of Congress and end up in jail, therefore nearly everyone avoided this trap. The object of the exercise was to get witnesses to name names. The committee's justification was that unless a person named others, how was the committee to know how sincere the witness was when claiming they no longer had ties to the party?

Imagine the excitement when Cvetic delivered a list of 300 plus names! The media hysteria that followed was exactly what FBI Director Hoover wanted. The process of criminalizing membership in the party was completed when Cvetic, under oath, told stories about the structure of the party, what it was trying to do, and who was helping them do it. The subversive aspects of the party were revealed by Cvetic and he got attention in the national press for his efforts.

Of all the hundreds of individuals who had appeared before UHAC and other committees, Cvetic had the most profound knowledge of the background of the party, its members, and even the philosophy of Karl Marx. Cvetic put a face on the anti-God and anti-religion attitude of communism. It was Hoover's line that communism was anti-American. Cvetic revealed the inner workings of the party's security apparatus and how they spied on each other, including him. Instead of some innocent 'dupe', the committee had a first-hand account of membership in the party from *an official FBI undercover agent.* In many ways, Cvetic was the confirmation Hoover needed to convert the skeptics. Cvetic's testimony stressed that the Communist Party was not just a political party but also an agent of a foreign power that had unfriendly intentions. This was crucial testimony at the time.

Cvetic lit a fuse. He was the brave undercover FBI agent who had to make his own luck for nine years. The task confronting Cvetic, by his own admission, was beyond his own imagining. His public appearances helped convince the public there was something real to fear from the Communist Party, and that the only certainty was that the problem would get worse.

As for the cynics and critics of Cvetic, about all we can ask is: Why is anybody not the best possible person he might be?

———

For many years Cvetic lived in a hotel in Pittsburgh. He admitted to moving into the William Penn Hotel in 1945. He had various pseudonyms and used "Bob Stanton" as his hotel name. It appears from reports that Cvetic lived there at an extremely favorable rate. One report has him living there "gratis." Cvetic himself gave different versions of this, so it is impossible to know for sure who was paying for it, if anyone. The hotel's manager had claimed that he knew Cvetic was an agent for the FBI and bragged about moving him from floor to floor during the period 1945 to 1950. One thing is known for sure: He did not have the money to pay the room rates, even though he did have a license to sell insurance and used his contacts at the CP to drum up clients.

Cvetic told his comrades in the CP that he was forced to live in the hotel because his own mother and family did not want him in their home unless he renounced his communist ties. Cvetic claimed one of the most terrible moments in his life was the death of his mother who died, he said, without ever being told that Matt was not a Communists but an FBI undercover agent.

Contrary to some reports I have read, Cvetic was a trusted member of the party up until the time he left. Although after he surfaced, Nelson and others claimed that they had been aware of his FBI snitching for some months, a desperate brag, no doubt. Most assuredly, had they been aware of his FBI affiliation, they certainly would not have let him leave CP headquarters with nearly a hundred pounds of documents, including the party's bank statements, minutes of meetings, correspondence, confidential notes, and names and addresses of members and fellow travelers. Just prior to Cvetic's appearance at HUAC, he dumped the boxes of materials on their desks.

Cvetic surfaced because he could not stand the hurt his family had endured any longer. As the Cold War intensified and the Soviet Union slammed down on the Eastern European countries, the Soviet domination of the Slovenian states over the Roman Catholic religion took its toll in western Pennsylvania. American Catholics tied communism to un-godliness and communists were vilified. Communists were about as welcomed in those communities as a whore in church. Family members threatened and pleaded with Cvetic to end his ties. And so he did.

Cvetic disagreed with the Bureau over the issue of how the break was to take place. Cvetic wanted the FBI to announce it. They refused. He thought it was necessary for the FBI to make a clear statement that he was a good citizen and had been following instructions for the nine years he was undercover. Hoover, however, did not want to assist Cvetic in using his relationship with the FBI for self-promotion. Therefore, he refused Cvetic's request. Hoover did later agree that if and when Cvetic was called to testify about matters of which he had knowledge, that they would refer to him as "an agent of the FBI" and not an ex-communist willing to tell all. On January 23,1950 it was official: Cvetic was a civilian again without any ties to the FBI or the CP. Throughout the Pittsburgh press the separation was treated as something that occurred by "mutual agreement".

"I Was a Communist for the FBI" is the movie that resulted from Cvetic's newfound fame, starring Frank Lovejoy as Matt Cvetic. A radio show featuring Dana Andrews as Cvetic ran from April 23, 1952 until October 14, 1953. The show had an incredible budget of $12,000 a week, an amount unheard of to produce a radio show during that period. The show always ended with Andrews as Cvetic saying, "I am a Communist for the FBI, I walk alone."

The *Saturday Evening Post* series about Cvetic ("as told to Pete Martin") led to the movie.

———

Cvetic's first appearance at the HUAC followed by one month Senator Joseph R. McCarthy's speech to a Republican's women club at the McClure Hotel in Wheeling, West Virginia. The testimony of Cvetic and the resulting media frenzy brought the subject to the top of the agenda (Bureau, The secret history of the FBI, Kessler, 2002). "While I cannot take time to name all the men in the State Department who have been named as members of the Communist Party and members of a spy ring, I have here in my hand a list of 205-a list of names that were known to the secretary of state and who, nevertheless, are still working and shaping policy of the State Department," McCarthy said. That number was never heard again. Later that same week he said the correct number was 57. One wonders if he was looking at a bottle of ketchup.

No single number was ever agreed upon, and although the FBI made every effort to back up McCarthy, it failed in doing so. One of the threats that resulted from what McCarthy did was that he distracted and took away from Cvetic's credibility and others like him who were telling a more or less true story based upon their personal experiences.

By 1954 Hoover tired of McCarthy and the Bureau stopped helping him. During the Army-McCarthy hearings of 1954, McCarthy failed once again to pinpoint where the communists were who he alleged were serving in the U.S. Army. McCarthy's career ended with the hearings sixty days later. On December 2, 1954, the Senate voted to censure McCarthy. On May 2, 1957, McCarthy died. He was only forty-seven.

2

THE END JUSTIFIES THE MEANS

"Even a majority enjoys no real immunity from the modern forms of psychological warfare which governments use to coerce consent. Nowadays large majorities can be manipulated by carefully timed headlines, revelations, and a thoroughly unscrupulous exploitation of the silence and secrecy surrounding many phases of government," wrote Carey McWilliams in his book, "Witch Hunt". There was a time in America when Communism was portrayed as an idealistic form of liberalism. Some even characterized it as 20th Century Americanism. But the real secrets of communism were not known until Cvetic and others like him began telling their stories in public.

Cvetic's message was, in a nutshell, that with the Communists, the end justified the means. In this mindset, it was perfectly fine to lie, cheat, steal, harm, kill, spy or do whatever it required to reach the goal of communism. This was a far different view of communism than was being fostered in the liberal media where the CP was seen as a political party with great egalitarian ideals.

In honest retrospect, what were the Hollywood Ten fighting for? Was it really racial equality? None of them moved into ghettos. Was it working for a new redistribution of the wealth? Did it really want the workers to take over? Not hardly. These people were driving the latest model convertibles, living in lavish Beverly Hills homes and catering parties that cost more in one day than a worker made in a year. All in all, as a group, they had no distaste for living as high as possible. One writer, Richard Rovere, wrote, "The investigators and the investigated have seemed richly to deserve each other."

But if we dismiss HUAC as publicity hounds, we lose the seriousness of the purpose of the hearings.

Cvetic was a witness that brought sympathy with him and not anger. He was not a combatant. He was there voluntarily. He wanted to tell his story. He placed himself in the center of political disagreements. He did not need a lawyer sitting at his side to advise him to protect his rights. He gave up his rights, in his own view, when he joined the CP for the FBI.

HUAC had not had much luck penetrating the inner workings of Communist Party front groups or organizations until Cvetic testified. The tactic the communists had used of locating a leader or celebrity with no known leftist leanings and persuading them to endorse a pet cause was brilliant in many ways. It became tremendously successful until how it was done was revealed, and then everyone was alerted to the techniques used by the CP and all were left wary.

These so-called humanitarian pressure groups would sign a petition to champion the release of a person "wrongfully imprisoned" or were asked to gather political support for a certain social cause or advance "Negro Rights", unaware that they were actually endorsing a Communist propaganda vehicle. Such persons or groups would then unwittingly be backing the CP. From the viewpoint of the party, it was a great idea as it was far better having five, six or 10 groups showing interest in the same subject than just the CP. Cvetic told how it would happen.

He was key in the development of radio programs that were propaganda messages disguised as social conscience. The CP produced the programs in western Pennsylvania in the languages familiar to Cvetic. These programs were then shopped around to the numerous stations that reached the various ethnic communities, however they were packaged as programs sponsored by some organization, such as the National Negro Congress or American Committee for the Defense of the Foreign Born. The stations had no idea the shows were produced by the CP.

Cvetic also disclosed how the party created fictitious front groups with such objectives as achieving racial and social justice, assistance for those wrongfully accused, and so forth. Creating such front groups was not easy. He said that leaders of these types of organizations were "cultivated" by Steve Nelson or Roy Hudson, both district organizers, and that Nelson and others would call on the organization asking for their support of whatever cause he was peddling that day. Very often a priest or minister was the object of this approach, according to Cvetic.

"It is the duty of a Communist to join as many organizations as he or she possibly can, and this was twice as important if the commie was a teacher, nurse, physician, lawyer, etc. The goal is that each member join at least ten other organizations and this is the way the commies get their message out, and infiltrate into legitimate organizations," Cvetic testified. "This was later very helpful if the commies wanted to support a certain local political candidate or referendum, as there were members in these groups to try to gather the support of several groups that would influence the public."

According to Cvetic, the CP was successful using these methods to infiltrate and control such organizations as the Croatian Fraternal Union, a group he had had close contact with during his party membership. "The objective was to have these groups in place so that when we needed them, we may be able to turn issues into Jewish issues, Negro issues, Slovenian issues, and of course this was what Nelson concentrated on with help from other members."

Another group catching the eye of the CP in western Pennsylvania, according to Cvetic, was the Labor Youth League. Cvetic managed to get away from the CP with important documents demonstrating its activism within the organization. Cvetic said that the group was under the control of the western Pennsylvania CP since 1949. All the educational materials used by the group had racial themes but themes of harmony and working together to solve problems of unemployment, creating jobs, freedom and peace. Unemployment was very bad, especially among blacks, and foreign minorities, and the CP tried to take advantage of their disadvantage by depicting itself as a friend in need, and one that will walk with them hand and hand to correct the inequities. "Commies made strong efforts to recruit Negroes," Cvetic said, "but we were not that successful in recruiting Negro leaders."

Not all the activities involving the emerging "Red Scare" took place in western Pennsylvania. Within one year of Cvetic's first open testimony that rocked the country with his firsthand stories of 'commies' and their subversive tactics, the nation slipped into a period of intense hunting for Communists. Consider the following timetable: (Remember Cvetic began his testimony in January of 1950 but it continued into February, grabbing one headline after the other.)

January 21, 1950: Alger Hiss convicted of perjury in denying that he passed secret documents to Communist agent Whittaker Chambers

February 2, 1950: Klaus Fuchs arrested

March 1950: Julius Rosenberg warns Greenglass to flee country

<u>May 1950:</u> Rosenberg asks his physician about what kind of shots are necessary for trip to Mexico

<u>May 22, 1950:</u> Harry Gold confesses to the FBI

<u>May or June 1950:</u> Rosenbergs visit a photographer to obtain passport photos

<u>June 15, 1950:</u> David Greenglass names Julius as the man who recruited him to spy for the Soviet Union

<u>June 16, 1950:</u> Julius Rosenberg is first interviewed by FBI

<u>June 30, 1950:</u> United States forces engage in the Korean War

<u>July 17, 1950:</u> Julius Rosenberg arrested

<u>August 11, 1950:</u> Ethel Rosenberg arrested

<u>August 1950:</u> Sobell and family are kidnapped by Mexican thugs and delivered to U. S. authorities at border

<u>January 31, 1951:</u> Grand jury indicts Rosenbergs, Sobell, David Greenglass, and Yakolev

<u>February 1951:</u> Greenglasses change their story, implicating Ethel Rosenberg in spy activities

<u>March 6, 1951:</u> Trial begins

<u>March 15, 1951:</u> William Perl is arrested on espionage charge

<u>March 28, 1951:</u> Trial ends

<u>March 29, 1951:</u> Jury returns verdict: Guilty of conspiracy to commit espionage

For your information, here is the statement made by the U.S. attorney when the jury was turned in:

"The conviction of the defendants in a criminal case is no occasion for exultation. It has been said that the Government never loses a case—because if there is a conviction the guilty are punished, and if there is an acquittal, the presumption of innocence must permanently prevail. The conviction of these defendants, however, is an occasion for sober reflection. That you the jury so considered it is evidence from the fact that

you deliberated for six and a half hours last night, and the nature of your requests as to the evidence and the identity of the witnesses amongst other things demonstrates that you complied throughout with the instructions of the learned Court; and that your conclusion is a mature, a reflected one . . .. The jury's verdict is a ringing answer of our democratic society to those who would destroy it. First, because a full, fair, open and complete trial—in sound American tradition—was given to a group of people who represented perhaps the sharpest secret eyes of our enemies. They were given every opportunity to present every defense and I would fight at all times for their right to defend themselves freely and vigorously. Secondly, your verdict is a warning that our democratic society, while maintaining its freedom, can nevertheless fight back against treasonable activities...."

<u>April 5, 1951:</u> Judge Kaufman imposes the death sentence on Rosenbergs, sentences Sobell to 30 years

This death sentence is not surprising. It had to be. There had to be a Rosenberg Case because there had to be an intensification of the hysteria in America to make the Korean War acceptable to the American people. There had to be hysteria and a fear sent through America in order to get increased war budgets. And there had to be a dagger thrust in the heart of the left to tell them that you are no longer gonna give five years for a Smith Act prosecution or one year for Contempt of Court, but we're gonna kill ya! **Julius Rosenberg, as quoted by his attorney, Emanuel Bloch, September 22, 1953.**

<u>Note:</u> **This defense attorney's summation clearly shows that he knows and understands the attitude of the times about communists:**

SUMMATION OF EMANUEL BLOCH FOR THE DEFENSE (EXCERPTS)

"The fear that an impartial jury could not be secured was particularly important in this type of case. Now, all of you are New Yorkers or you come from the environs of New York. We are a pretty sophisticated people. People can't put things over on us very easily. We are fairly wise in the ways of the world and the ways of people and we all know that there is not a person in this world who hasn't some prejudice, and you would be inhuman if you didn't have some prejudice. But we ask you now as we asked you before, please don't decide this case because you may have some bias or some prejudice against some political philosophy.

"If you want to convict these defendants because you think that they are Communists and you don't like communism and you don't like any member of the Communist Party, then, ladies and gentlemen, I can sit down now and there is absolutely no use in my talking. There was no use in going through this whole rigmarole of a three weeks' trial. That is not the crime.

"But believe me, ladies and gentlemen, I am not here, other defense counsel are not here as attorneys for the Communist Party and we are not here as attorneys for the Soviet Union. I can only speak for my father and myself. We are representing Julius and Ethel Rosenberg, two American citizens, who come to you as American citizens, charged with a specific crime, and ask you to judge them the way you would want to be judged if you were sitting over there before twelve other jurors..."

Julius and Ethel Rosenberg were charged with the crime of conspiracy to commit espionage, and tried under the Espionage Act of 1917. The trail leading up to their arrests was a complex web of espionage, defection, code-breaking and confession. On July 17, 1950, Julius Rosenberg was arrested, three weeks later, on August 11, 1950, his wife Ethel Rosenberg. They were imprisoned in the New York House of Detention. They were found guilty of conspiracy to commit espionage on March 29, 1951, and sentenced to death on April 5, 1951. They were executed on June 19, 1953.

This book is not about Alger Hiss or Whittaker Chambers or the spy case of the Rosenbergs. If you are reading this book, we are assuming you have some knowledge about these cases. Our point here is that if you want to understand the beginning of the great 'red scare', you have to understand Matt Cvetic and mark his testimony as the genuine beginning of it. The support of law enforcement was never higher than it was following Cvetic's revelations and the public's demand to identify and punish Communist spies was at its peak. Is it really any wonder so many anti-Communist movies were made during that period, including Cvetic's?

Now let's begin to look into some of the actual undercover duties taken on by Cvetic in his role as a mole in the CP for the FBI. We will do what others have not done in writing about Cvetic, we will reveal, as best we can, the information in some of his files.

3

CVETIC'S FILES

Matt Cvetic had records from more than 3,000 Communist Party meetings he attended as an agent for the FBI. Some of the information was divulged when he went public at the UHAC hearings but we will never know what secret information was held back by orders of the FBI. Certainly there were many reports and even names that they did not wish Cvetic to expose. This is the primary reason Cvetic's legacy will never be safe from the confusions of history. However, as years went by, Cvetic passed on more and more to the public in articles, interviews, and through his hundreds of speaking engagements. He did not make public the names of Soviet secret police and Soviet spy agents that he had reported to the FBI.

There are people who declare they knew Cvetic was an undercover agent for the FBI but it is highly unlikely he ever told anyone himself, other than the Roman Catholic priest in his parish where he was well-known. In Cvetic's own book, *The Big Decision,* he tells of his relationship with Father Daniel Lawless. According to Cvetic, Lawless blessed him and bestowed a "special dispensation to give up attending Mass and receiving sacraments." Lawless confirmed Cvetic's version of this disclosure in an interview, claiming he frequently prayed with Matt and consoled him during episodes he feared being exposed by his comrades. Lawless said Cvetic was terrified at times, and he sought comfort in his religion and with his priest.

Roman Catholics were ardent anti-Communists at this time and had been for many years prior to Cvetic surfacing. The Knights of Columbus is one of numerous Catholic organizations publishing a list of 'approved' movies and entertainment, and they focused on disapproving amusements they deemed were tinged red. The *Pittsburgh Catholic* was flagrantly anti-Communist, as were many of the other Catholic press. Taking into consideration this culture and Cvetic's upbringing, we can only suppose how difficult it was at times for Cvetic to sustain his public role as an avowed Communist. He confessed he felt enormous guilt and disgrace for his connection with the Communists Party. The issue for him became nothing less than survival.

It is too laborious and only inflates our purpose here to study every file that was left by Cvetic in terms of the meetings he disclosed to the FBI. It is, however, crucial to discuss some of them, so that we can make an effort to experience the power of fear that Cvetic felt from time to time. The CP painted a picture of an American society on the brink of collapse. Cvetic described the meetings as "a quagmire of verbosity, where the significant was overlooked in favor of the trivial."

Cvetic's Files

In one instance, Cvetic relates his orders to go to an exclusive resort to pass counterfeit money. "It was like living on the brink of a volcano. Inside are the ruins, the price I paid for being a communist for the FBI." To carry out the orders, the party acquired expensive luggage, lent Cvetic a diamond ring and other jewelry, and dressed him in the best clothes they could find. The CP desired to see if he was willing to do it, for one thing, as a loyalty test; and they also enjoyed "exchanging some bad money for good," according to Cvetic. When he advised the FBI what he was asked to do, his contact encouraged him, much to Cvetic's surprise. It appears that it was not news to the FBI that the Communists did counterfeiting. They were hopeful that Cvetic uncovered who the engravers were and where they were to be found. He states that he did. While these were not supposed to be kamikaze missions, at times he felt they were planned that way.

One of the more fascinating cases discussed by Cvetic was a trip he was ordered to take by train to San Diego, where he connected with other operatives of the party for the purpose of offering assistance in smuggling "23 trained saboteurs" from Eastern Europe into the United States. Cvetic was chosen since he had knowledge of the languages. Unfortunately for Cvetic, he did not have time to notify his FBI contact in Pittsburgh about the operation. During the entire period Cvetic worried that he could not call the FBI, so he decided to find another way to draw their attention to him. After being in Tijuana for two days, and growing in concern for his lack of support from the FBI, he convinced his handler it was risky to try to bring those 23 individuals across the border because they all had blue eyes, blond hair and very fair complexions. He convinced his handler that this would never work, and that they must be made up to look darker, like Mexicans. After a day or so of mulling it over, Cvetic was allowed to go shopping for the dye and stain he needed.

Realizing that federal agents of all types from the USA and Mexico closely policed the border town, Cvetic let it be known that he needed many cans of stain and bottles of dye. He deliberately acted suspiciously, talking nervously and loud. He made several trips to places to shop before making the return to each to actually make purchases of large quantities of the supplies. By doing so, he did successfully attract the attention of law enforcement. He told them who he was and why he was there. The FBI was notified.

"I was free and at large, but things that I saw in the party, I hated," Cvetic said. None was worse than when he was asked to go to a high school in Pittsburgh to conclude the process of initiating the school principal into the Communist Party. Cvetic discussed the "revolutions" with him, and he listened as the principal bragged about how easy it is for a trained party member to offer the doctrine of the party to young people. "I left there with what felt like a great knot in my stomach."

"Being a comrade to me was the most dangerous occupation in the world that I could have chosen." Consider the time he was to deliver a package to Canada that was in a locked box. An FBI contact met him aboard the train, opened the box, and discovered $500,000 in American money. It was not counterfeit. The money was to be used for paying workers to sabotage defense industry work projects. Cvetic was surprised the FBI agent simply closed up the box and told him to proceed. "Aren't you going to swap this for counterfeit or take it away or something?" He was told that it was more essential to find out about the person in Canada who ended up with the money. "Give us a call when you get the information, we will then pass it on to the Canadian authorities."

Cvetic received a tour of the Caribbean, paid for by the Communist Party. On one of the islands, the mission was to hand over a folder full of money to a high-level government official. When Cvetic saw that the recipient was the general in charge of security for the island, he could not believe his eyes. "We have high hopes for this guy," his commie-traveling companion told him. Cvetic described the general as "charismatically evil."

As another test, Cvetic was given an order to visit a specific warehouse in the sleaziest part of town with a comrade he particularly did not like. Upon entering, he saw three Communist "goons" beating up someone. Eventually the goons left the subject for dead, joking that they would return later to make it look like a suicide. Cvetic knew that if what he saw was ever disclosed, he was one of only five suspects who could have revealed it. "I had to live with this all my life."

"Night was a time of fear." One morning Cvetic was awakened at 3 a.m. by hard knocks on his hotel room door. He was ordered to get dressed and to follow the two men who came for him. "I was afraid I had been found out, and that they were going to arrange my 'suicide'." He was taken to a location where he was told he was leaving for Chicago with two others for the purpose of assisting new arrivals from the Soviet Union who were brought in to take care of 'traitorous members'. This was, Cvetic said, another test. When they arrived in Chicago, they simply turned around to return to Pittsburgh.

In the Communist Party, "Things only seem to be what they seem to be," Cvetic wrote for one record. A fellow comrade instructed him that he was to join her in meeting a plane from Washington, D.C. A courier was scheduled to arrive with a portfolio of top-secret materials that they were to take to a man in a hotel in New York City. When he notified the FBI of his assignment, he was instructed that he should be present when the portfolio was delivered in New York. The FBI wanted to know the identity and location of the person, so that they would know how information was trafficked out of the country. The mission was complicated by the fact that the female Communist told Cvetic he would probably not be present when the package was turned over. He had to contact the FBI again to inform them that if they wanted him at the delivery, the FBI would have to arrange to get her out of the picture. This they did at the airport in New York, by having the local police arrest her on a 'mistaken identity' case.

At one point, Cvetic, at the end of his rope, was overwhelmed with fear. "I am about to crack," he told the FBI contact on the phone. "We better meet. Nine years of this is more than anyone can take." The fright arose when informed that a member of the local party just committed suicide. "I heard that he was suspected of being an FBI informant. If that was true, I may have been next." The FBI refused to confirm or deny that the dead person was an informant, but they did everything to quiet Cvetic down.

"Your nerves are shot, and that is all. You need a rest, maybe, a break. We can't tell you anything about that man, except that we regret he is dead. What you have to do, if you don't want to be next, is pull yourself together," the FBI agent told him.

"I never felt so alone. I wanted to call my mother. I wanted her to know the truth about me. I thought the end was coming."

Cvetic also contended with the likelihood that the FBI had other undercover agents also working on some of the same assignments, and it was also possible that his contacts at the FBI in Pittsburgh knew nothing about it. This is the account of one of those assignments.

"As I was walking down a main street, a beautiful and well dressed woman came alongside of me and told me to join her for a taxi ride. I questioned her as to who she was, but she said it was party business and that I was expected to do what I was asked. I did." Cvetic was taken to a very exclusive high-rise apartment building where they exited the elevator at the penthouse floor. The woman had a key for the end suite, fully luxurious and surrounded by views of the city. A man sat on a couch and invited Cvetic to sit down beside him but before doing so, Cvetic demanded to know who they were. They told him nothing.

"We were told that you were a very disciplined member who followed orders. Just do what we tell you," the man said. Cvetic was ordered to Toronto to meet someone yet unnamed and un-identified who was to give him an envelope. He was to return to Pittsburgh with the envelope and telephone this penthouse apartment upon his return. Cvetic balked at the orders. He demanded they be confirmed by the local party leader. He was told he could tell no one about the orders, including the party head with whom he wanted to confirm the orders.

"I was worried and scared. Who were these people? They gave me my tickets for Toronto and an envelope with a generous amount of cash for expenses. They told me to leave the penthouse, hail a taxi, and go directly to the airport, speaking to no one." He hailed the taxi but realizing he was being followed, he eventually outmaneuvered the car behind them so that he could stop at CP headquarters to notify the leader.

The leader was distressed at what Cvetic told him but acknowledged that he did not know anything about the people or the penthouse. He advised Cvetic that the couple could be "counter-revolutionaries" or even FBI agents and that he should do exactly what he was told and report back to him when he returned from Canada.

After leaving the CP headquarters, he stopped at a pay phone to call his contact at the FBI. Cvetic asked if it were possible that he was dealing unknowingly with FBI undercover agents. His contact said he had no way of knowing but gave him the same advice the party leader gave him: Do what he was told and do it very carefully. He did.

Never did he find out who the two mysterious people were.

Yet an added bizarre story is the one Cvetic told about an imported crate of tuna. He was told to report to a seafood company to be found near the river docks. When he arrived there that night at the allotted time, he was let in to a warehouse, that had no visible signs of business operations. Cvetic was informed that a very important crate was to arrive soon and that it was his assignment to meet the customs officials and to sign for the crate. It was a crate of tuna cans and the cans had in them very important microfilm plans of "red action," or what the Communists called "proletariat intervention".

At 8:00 a.m. the next morning he was there to sign for the crate, but it had not arrived. He was shown a manifest that claimed that the crate had become very damaged in handling and had to be thrown overboard. Of course, Cvetic was reluctant to give this report to his superiors as he feared they may not have trusted him sufficiently, and may suspiciously believe he had the tuna cans and the microfilm. But when he told what happened, there were no surprised faces in the room. "Don't worry, comrade, we know it is not your fault. We have pre-planned that the crate be thrown over at a specified place to avoid any detection by the customs inspectors". He was told approximately where the crate was dropped and that he could hire divers to retrieve it. A boat was being made available to him later that night.

Cvetic notified the FBI. They retrieved the crate. The "goons" who did the "physical work" of the party, picked up the comrade, who was ordered to throw it over the side. He was answerable for Cvetic's inability to recover the crate. Unfortunately, Cvetic heard later that the seaman hanged himself.

————

FBI Director Hoover had ordered all of his field offices to do everything possible to secure wiretaps to confirm human contact information, such as those derived from undercover agents, like Matt Cvetic. By law, the FBI did not have jurisdiction to investigate communist organizations in the United States. He explained this to President Franklin D. Roosevelt. A loophole was found, and the plan proceeded to penetrate as many Communist organizations as possible.

Using the Nazi invasion of Poland on September 1, 1939 as an excuse, Hoover requested that Attorney General Murphy notify all police jurisdictions that they were to refer "any information obtained pertaining to espionage, counterespionage, sabotage, and neutrality regulations" to the FBI. From that moment on, for all practical purposes, the FBI assumed responsibility for investigating possible subversive organizations. Thus the FBI became officially, even if not strictly legally, the agency responsible for national security.

Nearly immediately, Hoover pleaded for additional funding and Congress responded by authorizing the hiring of several hundred new agents, additional legal and other staff, and more offices, of course. Hoover is said to have gone so far as to create a list of persons who were prospects for a "concentration camp," in the event of a national emergency. This led to the creation of files on virtually every person or any person that the FBI chose to have an interest in, notwithstanding any legitimate reason.

The number of agents in the Bureau increased from 353 in 1933 to 4,380 in 1945. Staff employees increased from 422 to 7,422. But was all of this wrong? Not if the consequences to national security are considered. The need was further stressed when on September 5, 1945, Igor Gouzenko, a Soviet cryptographer assigned to the embassy in Ottawa, Canada, defected. Gouzenko told stories of how the Soviets were planning to organize spy networks throughout Canada and the United States. And if Gouzenko was a gift, Elizabeth Bentley turned out to be Christmas.

Bentley appeared in the office of the FBI in Connecticut in late 1945. She told the agents that she had been employed with Soviet Intelligence for many years, and that she had frequently been exposed to highly classified materials, which she carried from American government employees who were spying against the United States. These employees worked in virtually every intelligence organization in the United States, including the War Department and various other departments of the government. She had studied at Columbia University and became a spy at the urging of her new husband, a KGB officer.

Bentley was actually turned in by a fluke. One night, following the death of her husband, she met a man in a Manhattan bar, got drunk, and had sex with him. Before leaving the hotel room, she searched the man, finding an employee badge for the "U.S. Probation Department." She wrongly deduced the man was a FBI agent, and that they had identified her as a spy. She thought about it, and then turned herself in. She disclosed that at least twice a month, she picked up documents and microfilm in Maryland and carried it to the KGB. Such revelations fueled the expansion of the FBI, and its interest in possible subversive activities.

Nothing much came of the Bentley case, but she was asked to give names of questionable individuals and she did. The FBI immediately began surveillance and other tactics and those named were actually discovered. By the time the FBI got around to trying to build a case, there was nothing to build it on except Bentley's word. Today, Bentley would be asked to serve as a counterspy for the purpose of building a legal case.

During this period of Cvetic's undercover work, there was a growing and verified threat of Communism to national security. While the public has always had an enthrallment with spy cases, it was not until Cvetic's revelations that they heard from an ordinary person, some of the plans attempted and carried out in the hopes of the ultimate victory of communism.

MATT CVETIC
Courtesy of Pittsburgh Post-Gazette

R.E. "Gus" Payne

4

MASTERS OF PUBLIC RELATIONS

"Since its inception, the Communist Party, USA, has been unswerving in its allegiance to the Soviet Union, which is committed to the goal of world domination by Communism. Because the United States is the principal deterrent to further Communist expansion, the Communist Party, USA, is, and will continue to be a serious threat to our internal security."

J. Edgar Hoover, 1962

By the mid-1950s membership in the Communist Party USA stood at only about 5,000, a decrease of approximately 75,000 from when Cvetic surfaced at his first UHAC in early 1950. The UHAC hearings and the publicity about communist subversion were a major break down on the party.

By now you may be asking, well, how did Cvetic become so well-known? Here is the account as it can be established from Cvetic's own writing, his personal appearances and his testimony at hearings. As early as 1947, Cvetic initiated a casual relationship with a newspaper reporter, James Moore, a city hall beat reporter employed by the Pittsburgh Sun-Telegraph. Introducing himself as Bob Stanton, Cvetic befriended the amiable reporter and eventually, revealed to him that he did some undercover work for the FBI. He did not reveal his secret entirely but he gave Moore enough bait to make him fish.

Moore and his paper were fascinated, but as Moore learned more and more that Cvetic's relationship with the FBI and the CP was long and complex, Moore, his editors and Cvetic reached a decision that the most they could do was an exclusive interview, assuming the FBI collaborated. In other words, the paper did not want to get caught up with the whole Communist underground thing that Cvetic alleged, unless the FBI verified Cvetic's status as an undercover agent. Moore, frustrated he was not going to break the story, introduced Cvetic to Pittsburgh's most strident anti-Communists, Blair F. Gunther and Harry Alan Sherman. At the time of their first meeting, Gunther was known as a 'hard-nosed' Allegheny

County judge. Earlier in his career, however, Gunther had been linked with Communist front groups.

Gunther rose to become "one of the most powerful men in Pennsylvania's Republican Party," according to his obituary in the New York Times. While Gunther's avowed anti-communism was seen as political opportunism by his enemies, his nearly ceaseless self-promotion resulted in complimentary stories in the local media. Cvetic was awed by him and appreciated that Gunther rose up from an Eastern European immigrant family. Gunther was a great spokesman for the anti-Communist Polish community in Pennsylvania. Also, Gunther and Cvetic were both fluent in Polish.

Gunther was, in fact, one of the most substantial individuals Cvetic had ever known. Gunther even headed up many local and national Polish organizations, and later became involved with Cvetic in the American Slav Congress. In 1954 Cvetic referred to the American Slav Congress as a "Communist controlled Communist front working on Slavic groups."

Gunther's past fascination with Communism had ended. He eventually became known as a fierce opponent of the ideology, but his past cost him dearly. He ran for judge as a Republican in 1950. His Democratic opponent charged that Gunther had ties to Communist front organizations, specifically, the American Slav Congress. Gunther retaliated by issuing a statement to the media that this charge was not true, that in fact he was an undercover agent for the FBI! He swore that if it became necessary, he will produce letters from the FBI to prove it. In the meantime, Hoover notified the attorney general that Gunther's claim was untrue. In the end, it did not matter as Gunther won the election. Apparently there were no letters backing up Gunther's claim that he was an undercover agent for the FBI.

Harry Alan Sherman was a very close friend and political supporter of Gunther. He was also an avid anti-Communist and a very fine attorney. He had a substantial income and was distinguished in the legal community in Pittsburgh as a great litigator and a fiercely patriotic speaker. Sherman and Gunther grew to be Cvetic's sponsors. They created an anti-communist group called "Americans Battling Communism" (ABC). It was this organization that paid Cvetic's expenses to Washington for his first appearance before the UHAC.

Gunther and Sherman pulled together a citywide meeting consisting of at least 50 notable citizens to form what they called "the Pittsburgh plan against Communism." Their charter for ABC was filed in late 1947 and they were later classified as a legal non-profit corporation. Sherman and Gunther perceived in Cvetic a lightening rod to enhance credibility to ABC, as well as help it become a force in anti-communism in the United States. Cvetic sought the chance to surface with dignity, using other peoples' money, and the opportunity to tell his story to the world. Moore was pleased he had made a good match.

As ABC took form, many other important figures in Pennsylvania became active in the organization, giving it even more status: Joseph Barr, a state senator, and official in the Allegheny County Democratic Party; William Burns, a radio station executive; Judge Harry Montgomery; and Deputy Attorney General Raymond Evans. With their help, ABC tapped resources in labor unions, ethnic organizations and other anti-Communist groups. In time, Judge Musmanno assumed de facto leadership as the chief spokesman for ABC.

Cvetic owed his debut to Sherman, Gunther, Moore and ABC.

Cvetic's surfacing was a brilliant public relations plan orchestrated by Moore, Sherman and Gunther. Before going national, Cvetic consented to tell a portion of his story to Gunther in the form of a legal deposition. With Moore's assistance, Gunther passed on the deposition to the Pittsburgh media. Cvetic's statement and story broke while he was en route to Washington for his first UHAC hearing. Needless to say, the press buzz swarmed Gunther, ABC and Cvetic who were then exposed to the national media.

Such highly developed preparation paid off, as Cvetic had taped a thirty-minute interview with Moore intended for broadcast on the radio while he was testifying at UHAC. Of course, the broadcast was very flattering of Cvetic, who was portrayed as an American hero for what he had done as an undercover FBI agent for nine years. The PR was brilliant, but certainly Cvetic deserves credit for making a strong appearance at UHAC, convincing many in the media of his heroic deeds.

Sherman got what he wanted: publicity. He was described in the deposition as one of the attorneys questioning Cvetic on behalf of the ABC. Cvetic explained the influence of the party in Slavic organizations and he foretold of the forthcoming "smear attacks" from the Communists planned against hard fighting anti-Communists Gunther and Sherman.

This author differs with conclusions drawn by Leab and others that as time went on, Cvetic "embellished" his story, even under oath, while testifying before various hearings. These writers justify their conclusions by believing that Cvetic, Gunther and Sherman continued to add to their stories, as the old ones told got stale. They also believe Hoover became concerned about Cvetic, although Hoover had never publicly questioned the veracity of Cvetic's reports.

In fact, Hoover was fretful about Cvetic and the truthfulness of his testimonies. He ordered the Pittsburgh office perform a thorough review of all of Cvetic's reports that dealt with subjects on which he had testified. The result? "Cvetic's testimony when considered on a broad basis and in its entirety, it is fairly accurate…" As might be expected, the report went on to say that while this was true, there were occasional "misstatements". Overall, however, the FBI office in Pittsburgh considered his testimony right on target with Cvetic's filed reports. The Pittsburgh Press summed it all up: "There has been no room for doubt at any time about the veracity of Cvetic."

Cvetic accepted that his immediate future was to live the life of an ex-Communist FBI informant. He also knew that he did not have the money or the means to do so without help. He arranged a contract with Sherman and Moore, requiring they help him, with Sherman acting as his "attorney-agent" and Moore as his "author-editor". Sherman and Moore promised to do everything within their power to promote what was then known as "The Cvetic Story."

The fees for Sherman and Moore were set at 30 percent each, certainly an unrealistic cut of whatever Cvetic made from his story and public appearances. Until early in 1952 when Sherman parted company with Cvetic, he did travel and appear with him before UHAC hearings as his attorney and often spoke for him to the media. Beginning with the nation's obsession with Cvetic and his story, Sherman and Moore tried to put together deals that would make them money. Their first major breakthrough was with the *Saturday Evening Post.*

To be published in three installments, *"I Posed as a Communist for the FBI"*, the Cvetic story as told to writer Pete Martin, kicked-off the national campaign for Cvetic. It got off to a great start. One of only a handful of major national publications, the *Saturday Evening Post* signed a contract with Moore and Sherman on March 20, 1950 for the exclusive rights to the story. The magazine paid $5,000, with an initial payment of $1,000 and the balance paid in installments. The articles were enormously flattering of Cvetic and Hoover's reviewers found nothing in them to complain about.

In fact, one report quotes the FBI as stating that "all references to the FBI were laudatory" and, in fact, the Bureau never looked better!

Following the publication of the articles, movie studios came calling. Warner Brothers purchased the movie rights to the story as it was told in the *Post*, for $12,500. Again, the agreement called for one initial payment and two installments. The amount paid is paltry by today's standards and was even in the 1950s when the going rates were $50,000 and more. Cvetic did not know the business and neither did Moore or Sherman, and as a result the deal was negotiated in favor of the studio. Of course, Cvetic had to split shares with Moore and Sherman, but he also agreed to adding Martin, the author of the *Post* series, who got cut in for 15 percent. Instead of hiring Cvetic as a consultant to the movie, Warner Brothers contracted with Martin, who they paid $500 a week plus living and travel expenses while the movie was in production.

There are more than a few contradictions with what Warner Brothers did. The reason they wanted to buy the story from the *Post* was they needed the insulation for doing a fact-based movie without having done any of the research themselves. It made their lawyers happy. But after going to such great lengths to obtain the rights from the magazine, they then took many liberties with the story, fictionalizing major parts of it. It is a complaint we hear even today from book authors who look up at the screen and say they do not recognize their book. This was not Cvetic's fault. What was his fault was allowing these interlopers to take advantage of him. This adds credibility to the fact that Cvetic once said that the most money he ever made in his life in one year was $15,000.

Warner Brothers' version added a romance that did not take place and there is hardly any language from the magazine that ended up in the movie. They even changed the title from *I Posed as a Communist for the FBI* to *I Was a Communist for the FBI*. The studio, after many trials and errors in scripts, contacted the FBI for assistance, but it was refused on the grounds that the studio did not contact them on a timely basis.

The movie premiered in Pittsburgh among great hoopla on April 19, 1951.

Frank Lovejoy portrayed Cvetic, but as a steelworker recruited by the FBI to infiltrate the union. The movie over-dramatizes Cvetic's double life by portraying his wife as a victim, when in fact he was already divorced. In the movie, Cvetic falls in love with a beautiful schoolteacher, a true

Communist, but with a naïve view of the world. There was no schoolteacher. There is not much reason to go into the details of the movie here, except to say that it is not truthful to the Cvetic story as told to the magazine.

Many writers refer to anti-Communist movies of this period as "propaganda films." Some go so far as to believe the promulgation of anti-communist films was an overreaction to the "red scare" days of UHAC and McCarthy. They may be right but the movie studios were not in the business of making movies to please the FBI or the government; they had to make money. Although we do not know how much money Cvetic's movie made, we do know it made the studio money.

The movie shaped an image of a tough talking hero whose personal sacrifices were great but whose determination and persistence helped defeat communism. National news and other magazines ran reviews, wrote articles and even published photos from the movie, giving Cvetic the public awareness he needed should he were to choose to make a career of fighting communism. Regardless of how well the movie was received, he was greeted warmly everywhere he spoke. Cvetic spent four to six weeks before the movie was released knocking on doors in the Northeast promoting the movie and himself. Warner Brothers picked up his travel expenses but paid him little for his efforts. However, he considered the time well spent as he opened up new contacts with newspersons in radio and with the newspapers.

Cvetic was also famous from the successful radio series that was broadcast on more than 600 stations once a week. Actor Dana Andews played Matt. Warner was paid $10,000 by the Ziv Company, a giant media conglomerate of the period, for the rights to the title; *I Was a Communist for the FBI.* Although a good deal for Cvetic's image, again his financial reward was very modest. Warner gave Cvetic only $4,000 out of the $10,000 but they did throw in $1,000 for him to go to Los Angeles where the show was scheduled for production.

It appears as though Cvetic let everyone take advantage of him. Ziv offered to pay him during 1952-1953 and pick up his expenses for lectures they set up to promote the radio shows. In 1958, Cvetic sued Ziv for $100,000, claiming they did not pay him what he was owed. A year or so later he settled for about $1,000. And if that was not bad enough, Sherman and Moore were convinced they were entitled to their share of the earnings from the radio series. Cvetic said he never agreed to pay but he was sued and lost. In the end, he only earned 27 percent of the income from the radio show; agents and lawyers got the rest.

Although television had stripped radio of many of its successful series, Ziv did a marvelous job of promoting the Cvetic series and they bragged how well it did financially. Ziv secured sponsors who wanted to be associated with anti-communism and in essence, the sponsors were able to take advantage of the publicity.

Ziv is the same company that discovered Herb Philbrick, a true FBI Special Agent who was undercover in Boston about the same time as Cvetic in Pittsburgh, and created a syndicated TV series called *I Led Three Lives*. While money flowed to Philbrick, and his career as a speaker and anti-communist blossomed, this was not the case with Cvetic. Yet, it seems now that Cvetic is the only one of the two undercover agents who penetrated the CP that is called a "paid witness", implying that Cvetic did what he did only for money, while Philbrick did what he did for love of country and FBI. (The most the FBI ever paid Cvetic was $100 a week!) If he did crave wealth, he certainly did not know how to achieve it. While it is probably true that Cvetic reached his peak as a professional anti-Communist the night of the premiere of the movie, he did manage to draw it all out nearly a decade.

R.E. "Gus" Payne

5

PUSHING FOR A NEW START

Leab frequently refers to Cvetic as a heavy drinker and womanizer. The most outlandish and improbable claim made is that Cvetic had to be put on a "two quart limit" per day ration. There is no basis for this assertion. Cvetic did like women and, yes, he enjoyed drinking but to declare that he devoured more than two quarts of liquor a day is totally ridiculous and a gross exaggeration. Family members and others who knew Cvetic said that toward the late 1950s Cvetic did acquire a reputation as a drinker but nothing anywhere approaching a two-quart a day drunk. Much of the bad information about Cvetic that has been written originated within Communist inspired sources. It is understandable why they would not like him.

Although Cvetic owned up to a drinking problem, and that he had even attended AA meetings, FBI agents in Pittsburgh who knew him over a 10 year period did not think at any time that his drinking was such a problem that it prevented him from doing his job. To the contrary, their reports on Cvetic were favorable, as we have already discussed. Hoover would have dumped Cvetic in a New York minute, if there were even a hint of alcoholism.

Cvetic fought to create a life for himself. He even took a stab at politics, running in the Republican primary for the Congressional seat in 1954. Obviously building a campaign on his reputation as the FBI undercover agent raised interest but he did not win the primary. His campaign was entirely about Communism but the voters also had bread and butter issues on their minds.

Probing for a new start, he headed west to Nevada where he used his press contacts to launch himself as a speaker in 1955.Cvetic remained in contact with the FBI. FBI agents in Pittsburgh liked Cvetic; they thought he had gone to Las Vegas to work in the media. Cvetic's reputation was tarnished, however, when a former "FBI undercover observer" by the name of Harvey Matusow charged that Cvetic's testimony could not be trusted. Matusow must of thought the same of his own testimonies, as he disclosed that much of what he had said was not true. This concerned the FBI and Hoover who started backing off unconditional support for the whole string of "undercovers" who had testified at UHAC and other hearings.

For a brief period Cvetic was the editor of the *Las Vegas Independent,* a weekly, but the paper went out of business. He returned to Pittsburgh, continued his close ties to anti-Communist groups, spending his time speaking to any group that would hear him. He sought out other promotional opportunities but he had little success.

Cvetic continued writing his memoirs and even hired grammarians and writers to help with the project. When he told the FBI office in Pittsburgh that the manuscript was nearly ready, they wanted to read it but Hoover suggested they not do so, fearing that Cvetic would later either cry FBI censorship or brag that the FBI approved. In fact, the FBI did not want anything to do with the project except protect the identity of their agents and specific episodes in which they and Cvetic were involved. To further add complications, when Warner Brothers found out about the book, they warned that they might have financial rights they wanted to protect. It seems as though Cvetic just had bad luck when it came to making money!

The Boston publisher who had considered Cvetic's proposed manuscript, backed out of the deal, perhaps at the request of the FBI, but more likely out of fear of libel suits, as Cvetic fully intended to use real names and places with no attempt to disguise persons or places. He finally solved his problem by publishing the book himself in 1959 using the title *The Big Decision.* He had learned to take the path of least resistance: he changed the names and places. The FBI had no comment on the book.

Cvetic was annoyed that Herb Philbrick's memoir, *I Led Three Lives* became a best seller and the TV series did very well. He held the FBI responsible for this, claiming they backed Philbrick and not him. This did not help his relationship with Hoover. The FBI cut him off after the controversy and Cvetic probably never really understood why. It was, likely, the FBI that encouraged Doubleday to walk away from the Cvetic manuscript but Cvetic did not know the reason.

Disappointed and saddened by his life in Pittsburgh, he moved to Los Angeles in early 1958. He had no plans or job but was hopeful that he would hook up with some of California's anti-Communists or right-wing political organizations to gain a living. Upon arrival there, he wrote up a brochure about himself extolling his nine years of undercover work, the movie and the radio show. He asked for speaking engagements. He received local and favorable press from the *Los Angeles Times.* He told anyone who would listen that he was peddling his book and that several studios were looking the proposal over.

Cvetic actually did fairly well arranging speaking engagements and tours for which he was paid a fee and his expenses. He associated with many groups and patriotic organizations, using his contacts within these groups to further his speaking opportunities. These organizations also helped him promote his book by advertising it to their members. Cvetic claimed that sales exceeded 50,000 units by 1961 but here again, it is doubtful that Cvetic made much money, as the retail price of the book was only $1.00.

During this period there were no reports of excessive drinking, and for the first time since the early 1950s, Cvetic was doing better financially. Perhaps in the end he felt cheated, angry and sad. He had to be too many people. In hindsight, Cvetic became the prisoner of a fate he could not alter or escape. He died of a heart attack July 26, 1962 in Hollywood. His was a success story whose ending pleased no one. His obituaries were generally favorable and described his exploits in detail. Ben Cvetic, his brother, was convinced Matt was murdered by a communist who may have poisoned him while eating a sandwich. A coroner's report cleared what mystery there was up by claiming the cause of death was a 'significant arterial sclerosis', which caused a heart attack.

Looking back over Cvetic's life, it is this author's opinion that it is not fair to consider Cvetic an opportunist or to dismiss him as a "paid witness". His critics claimed he relished applause and longed for fame. Perhaps. The life he lived for nine years was horrible by any standard and it required considerable sacrifice. There were few days in his life during those years that he did not live in fear of being discovered. He had no escape or retreat. He devoted his life to the cause of gathering information for the FBI and by their own admission, he reported well, regularly and truthfully for the entire period. He led them to meeting rooms where the CP planted their wires; he gave them advance plans of sabotage; and he exposed the Pittsburgh cell of the Communist Party as doing all it could to infiltrate ethnic and other organizations. And through it all, Cvetic stayed loyal to his church, and confided in his parish priest, a priest who was loyal to Matt for all of his life.

R.E. "Gus" Payne

6

MOVIES AS PROPAGANDA

"One of the most pressing tasks confronting the Communist Party in the field of propaganda is the conquest of this supremely important propaganda unit (the movie), until now the monopoly of the ruling class. We must wrest it from them and turn it against them."(Willi Muenzenberg, 1925, Daily Worker).

While some efforts were made, the communists certainly did not have the success the anti-communists had in producing films for mass audiences. The movie about Cvetic was only one of many such movies. Consider the others:

Ninotchka, 1939. Released again 1947. Reappeared as a musical in 1957, re-titled Silk Stockings.

The Iron Curtain. 1948. From Canada.

Sofia. 1948. Defeating communists by stealing their scientists from them.

Bells of Coronado. 1949. Stars Roy Rogers in a Western movie with espionage as a theme.

Conspirator. 1949. Stars Elizabeth Taylor and Robert Taylor.

Guilty of Treason. 1949. A 'docudrama'about the life of Roman Catholic Cardinal Mindszenty.

The Woman on Pier 13. 1949. From Howard Hughes' with the original title "I Married a Communist".

The Red Danube. 1949. About a Soviet ballerina.

The Red Menace. 1949. Documentary style production about Communist threats.

Walk a Crooked Mile. 1949. More against FBI than Communists.

Communism. 1950. Armed Forces Information Film.

R.E. "Gus" Payne

I Was a Communist for the FBI. 1951. Based on Matt Cvetic's stories.

The Whip Hand. 1951. About biological warfare.

Artic Flight. 1952. Spy posing as innocent.

Assignment Paris. 1952. Thriller.

Atomic City. 1952. Infiltration of Communists.

Big Jim McLain. 1952. John Wayne as HUAC agent.

Diplomatic Courier. 1952. Spies.

The Hoaxsters. 1952. Documentary style.

The Red Snow. 1952. About Alaska events.

The Steel Fist. 1952. Roddy McDowall.

The Thief. 1952. Directed by Ray Milland.

Walk East on Beacon Street. 1953. Boston based spies.

My Son John. 1953. Communism.

Man on a Tightrope. 1953. From Elia Kazan.

Never Let Me Go. 1953. Clark Gable.

Runaway Daughter. 1953. Espionage.

Savage Drums. 1953. Communism in the tropics.

Savage Mutiny. 1953. Communism on an island.

Night People. 1954. Gregory Peck as a spy.

Prisoner of War. 1954. Korean War.

Trial. 1955. Communists in USA.

Communist Blueprint for Conquest. 1956. U.S. Government produced.

And many, many, others, far too numerous to mention.

" Red Baiting - in the sense of reasoned, documented exposure of Communist and pro-Communist infiltration of government departments and private agencies of information and communication - is absolutely necessary. We are not dealing with honest fanatics of a new idea, willing to give testimony for their faith straightforwardly, regardless of the cost. We are dealing with conspirators who try to sneak in the Moscow-inspired propaganda by stealth and double talk, who run for shelter to the Fifth Amendment when they are not only permitted but invited and urged by Congressional committee to state what they believe. I myself, after struggling for years to get this fact recognized, give McCarthy the major credit for implanting it in the mind of the whole nation." (The Necessity of Red Baiting, *The Freeman*, 1st June, 1953))

Not very long ago, the University of Southern California, honored the Hollywood Ten as victims of the Cold War and champions of the First Amendment. This is the same crowd that raised money for Daniel Ortega of the Sandinistas, without asking one question as to the number of persons who would have to die for his revolution in Nicaragua. The communist and anti-communist ideological wars may be over in the movies but the legacy of both are still with us.

"Joe McCarthy was unquestionably the most controversial man I ever served with in the Senate. The anti-anticommunists were outraged at his claims that some of the principals in the Truman and Roosevelt administrations actively served the communist causes.

"McCarthy was supported by a strong, nationwide constituency, which included among others, Joseph P. Kennedy, the father of John, Bob, and Edward. A variety of respected, creditable federal employees disturbed by security risks in the national government provided McCarthy with a steady stream of inside information.

"The liberals mounted a skillfully orchestrated campaign of criticism against Joe McCarthy. Under the pressure of criticism, he reacted angrily. It is probably true that McCarthy drank too much, overstated his case, and refused to compromise, but he wasn't alone in his beliefs." (No Apologies, Senator Barry Goldwater, 1979)

R.E. "Gus" Payne

7

THE COLD WAR AND MATT CVETIC

"It only took 23 Commies to overthrow Russia," FBI Director J. Edgar Hoover

Since we used so many pages on Cvetic and his work during the 1950s, it is important we highlight concurring events, so that we can demonstrate how anti-Communism thrived and how this helped Cvetic turn this into his career for at least two decades.

Senator Joseph R. McCarthy's anti-Communist crusade began less than three weeks after Alger Hiss's conviction in 1950. The Hiss case helped launch the 1950's McCarthy period. "The impact of the Hiss case on the movement of anti-communism to the center of the political stage can scarcely be exaggerated." the historian James V. Compton wrote in 1973. The focus was always the guilt or innocence of Alger Hiss. If Alger Hiss was guilty as charged, and passed government documents to the Soviet Union when he worked for the United States State Department in the 1930s, this proves President Franklin D. Roosevelt's New Deal had been infiltrated and compromised by Communist spies. If Hiss were innocent, his conviction had been a historic miscarriage of justice.

Alger Hiss, who lived for 47 years after his conviction, devoted those years to a quest for vindication. (He died in 1996 at the age of 92.) His government pension was restored to him in 1972, and he was readmitted to the bar in Massachusetts in 1974. He was never able to have his conviction overturned. Whittaker Chambers, Hiss's accuser, who died in 1961 at the age of 61, received posthumous honors from the Reagan administration: President Reagan awarded him the Medal of Freedom in 1984.

Since Hiss's 1950 conviction, more than two dozen books have examined the case with mixed results.

———

There are now two great nations in the world, which starting from different points, seem to be advancing toward the same goal: the Russians and

the Anglo-Americans. . . . Each seems called by some secret design of Providence one day to hold in its hands the destinies of half the world.

Alexis de Tocqueville, *Democracy in America* (1835)

Did he foresee the Cold War?

During the Second World War, the Western democracies were not comfortable about allying themselves with Stalinist Russia. When the war ended, it did not take long for this unwanted relationship to end. Over the next few years, the Soviets imposed communist regimes in its post-war occupation zones in East Europe and North Korea. In China, the end of civil war brought a huge slice of the human population under Communism, and mass execution of political opponents followed. As the 1940s progressed, the West decided to form a system of defensive alliances to prevent any further spread of Communism.

The Organization of American States was founded in 1945 to coordinate the foreign policy of the Western Hemisphere, while all the principle nations of West Europe and North America were joined into the North Atlantic Treaty Organization (NATO) in 1947. Across the south of Asia, two more American alliance systems, CENTO (Central Treaty Organization) and SEATO (Southeast Asia Treaty Organization), were established to contain possible Soviet expansion southward. By 1959, most of the non-Communist world had promised to be *anti*-communist as well. Many of the recently released Asian nations decided to explore an independent foreign policy instead. Neither Soviet nor Western, they considered themselves a third world which would rather not get dragged into other people's quarrels. Of course, many of the non-aligned nations had their own quarrels to pursue, and they found that the superpowers were happy to support them in order to gain another piece on the chessboard. Thus, with the Americans supporting Israel, the Soviets found that they could gain influence in the region by assisting Israel's Arab neighbors.

With most of the world's governments declaring themselves pro-Western in the ideological conflict, the Communists readily supported any insurgent movement against those governments. Whether some of these rebel movements were truly communist is subject to debate, but in the eyes of the world at the time, the phrase "communist insurgent" was redundant because each word always implied the other.

The alliance system began to unravel in 1959 when Communist insurgents came to power in Cuba, gaining their first foothold in the Western

Hemisphere and setting off a chain reaction of crises which came very close to bringing about a full nuclear exchange between the superpowers. A more visible result of the various Cuban crises is that hemispheric unity was shaken as several Latin American countries, principally Mexico, decided that snubbing Cuba was not worth the risk and maintained diplomatic and economic relations despite the objections of the United States.

Meanwhile, the Soviets lost major ground in 1960, when China broke away after bickering over interpretations of Marxist doctrine, taking Albania and North Korea with them. China then tested its first atomic weapon in 1964 and withdrew from the world stage to indulge in the purifying ritual of the Cultural Revolution. About the same time, France decided that it didn't like its foreign policy being dictated by the United States, so it tested its first atomic weapon in 1960, and withdrew from NATO in 1965. Although it was almost certain that the French would be found on the American side in the event of a general European war, until then the French would pursue a foreign policy, which was neither pro-Soviet nor pro-American but merely French.

A more substantial defeat for the Americans came with the fall of Indochina to the communists in 1975. This region was not exactly vital to American interests, but because the United States had fought a major war to prevent this from happening, the stakes were high, and the defeat was horribly demoralizing. The replacement of the pro-American dictatorship in Nicaragua by Communist rebels also depressed American confidence, as did the fall of the pro-American Shah of Iran in favor of a vehemently anti-western theocracy. In fact, because the Americans had begun the Cold War riding high with so many nations in its corner, just about every subsequent change of regime anywhere in the world sank American influence just a bit lower. By the mid-80s, it appeared that the US was clearly losing the Cold War.

Appearances were deceiving. While the Western economies prospered despite the military buildups, the cost of maintaining a massive military machine was crippling the inefficient Soviet economy. The attempts at reform came to little, too late, and in 1989, the Soviets were forced to cut loose their East European satellites. In 1991, the constituent republics of the Soviet Union declared their independence and the Soviet Union ceased to exist altogether.

The Cold War was over.

———

Communist spies were real. Individual Communists did succeed at stealing secrets. The notorious spy cases of the early cold war and the surfacing of Cvetic in 1950 bolstered the contention that, as J. Edgar Hoover maintained, "every American Communist was, and is, potentially an espionage agent of the Soviet Union." The ramifications of the cases enumerated by Cvetic alone were enormous. There is enough evidence, mainly from people who either confessed or were caught in the act, to make it clear that some American, British, and Canadian citizens in or near the Communist Party did spy for the Soviet Union and did so for political reasons.

Though the threat of espionage gained national attention through such events as UHAC hearings, sabotage was the prime concern of policymakers. They feared that communist-led unions might go on strike or otherwise impede the operations of the nation's vital defense industries. These fears were reality when Cvetic exposed such plans during his testimonies. During the Nazi-Soviet Pact period, Communist labor leaders had been involved in several highly publicized strikes in the nation's defense industries. Part of a nationwide organizing drive mounted by unions of all political persuasions, the work stoppages were supposedly triggered by economic grievances, but Cvetic enumerated example after example where it was also from a desire to impede the nation's war effort. Cvetic cited these strikes during the early years of the cold war as evidence that the party had tried to sabotage American rearmament.

Cvetic was a child of his age but he was more than that, he was one of those few great Americans in our history who came along just in time.

8

CONSEQUENCES

JOHN WAYNE-ACTOR

As the national mood increasingly turned to anti-communism for all the reasons previously covered, popular actor John Wayne struck a conservative anti-communist position in a speech that was printed March 23, 1951 in the *Los Angeles Times*.

"LOYAL ACTORS CALL FOR FILM INDUSTRY PURGE OF ALL SUBVERSIVES

Hollywood has treated the Communist menace in its midst "too lightly" and the time has come for the film industry to purge itself of subversive elements, according to Actor John Wayne, who today started his third term as president of the Anti-Red Motion Picture Alliance for the Preservation of American Ideals.

Speaking last night at the Alliance's eighth annual meeting, Wayne took Actor Larry Parks to task for waiting 10 years before making public confession that he was once a Communist Party member. Wayne said that his earlier statement that Parks' admission was "commendable" was a "snap comment" and that the long interval of silence on Parks' part was "not to his credit."

"Let no one say that a Communist can be tolerated in American society and particularly in our industry," Wayne declared. "We do not want to associate with traitors. We want patriotism and justice. We hate no one. We hope those who have changed their view will cooperate to the fullest extent. By that I mean names and places, so that they can come back to the fellowship of loyal Americans.

"The bankers and stockholders must recognize that their investments (in the movie industry) are imperiled as long as we have these elements in our midst," Wayne told the 1000 film workers, actors and writers Jammed into the Hollywood American Legion Auditorium."

R.E. "Gus" Payne

Wayne presented a check for $1000 to William B. Keene, 26, of Manhattan Beach, a law student at the University of California at Los Angeles, as the first annual James K. McGuinness Award for Outstanding Americanism shown by a student on an American college campus.

Keene told of his battle to keep Communists from establishing a foothold on the Westwood campus through appointments to the staff of the *Daily Bruin* while he was president of the university's student body in 1949.

Another speaker was Hollywood Columnist Hedda Hopper, who hit Parks, saying: "The life of one American soldier is worth all the careers in Hollywood. We must be careful lest we give sympathy to those who do not deserve it-and Parks certainly does not."

Selection from collection of speeches given by Ronald Reagan, this dealing with communists in Hollywood (and also how he met Nancy!):

"There were then forty-three labor unions in the picture business. A few were independents but most were affiliated with the American Federation of Labor. The Screen Actors Guild was one of the latter, as was the International Association of Theatrical and Stage Employees - better known as the stagehands' union or by its initials, IATSE. During the absence of so many of us during the war something new had come into being. Some of the unions had gotten together to organize what they called the "Conference of Studio Unions," also known as CSU. The rump CSU group was run by a man named Herb Sorrell, head of the studio painters' union, who set out with a plan to gain jurisdictional control over a group of workers within an IATSE branch called the Set Erectors. There were only about 350 set erectors in the whole industry but the CSU called a strike demanding that the studios recognize it as their exclusive bargaining agent. The IATSE told its members to cross the CSU picket lines and war broke out. Naturally, actors and actresses came to the officers of the Guild, asking us what they should do. When we held the meeting, it was obvious that the CSU strike was a phony. It wasn't meant to improve the wages and working conditions of its members, but to grab something from another union that was rightfully theirs.

"The gates of the studios soon became a bloody battleground of daily clashes between the people who wanted to work and the strikers and outside agitators brought in to help them. A union of waterfront workers headquartered in San Francisco suspected of having Communist affiliations sent mass pickets to aid the CSU strikers. Homes and cars were bombed and many people were seriously injured on the picket lines; workers trying to drive into a studio would be surrounded by pickets who'd pull open their car door or roll down a window and yank the worker's arm until they broke it, then say, "Go on, go to work, see how much you get done today." In the end, we beat 'em. The strike collapsed in February 1947. The decision by the Guild and several other unions to ignore the picket lines ultimately destroyed not only the strike but also the Conference of Studio Unions.

"Later, several members of the Communist Party in Hollywood who had been involved in the attempted takeover went public and described in intimate detail how Moscow was trying to take over the picture business. The California Senate Fact-Finding Committee on Un-American Activities, after a lengthy inquiry, confirmed that the strike was part of a Soviet effort to gain control over Hollywood and the content of its films. Although the principal leader of the strike told Congress that he had never been a Communist, investigators produced evidence that they said proved he was a secret member of the party, and a year later, national leaders of his union concluded he had "willfully and knowingly associated with groups subservient to the Communist Party."

"Not long after that, I accepted an invitation to fill a vacancy on the board of directors of the Hollywood Independent Citizens Committee of the Arts, Sciences, and Professions. The group, known to everybody by its initials, HICCASP, had come into being as a support group for President Franklin D. Roosevelt and was a respected and prestigious liberal organization that had attracted some of the best-known names in Hollywood. There were about sixty board members at the meeting, many of whom I didn't recognize, particularly the members of the executive committee, who were seated at a table facing the board members.

"Dore Schary, the head of MGM, was sitting next to me and I nudged him and said: "Where are all the people that used to be here, the heads of the other studios and so forth?" He looked at me and then leaned over and whispered: "Stop by Olivia de Havilland's apartment after the meeting." Olivia was a member of the executive committee of HICCASP. Ten of us met later that night at her apartment and I was amazed when she and others in the room said they suspected Communists were trying to take over the organization. I'd previously decided that as a new board member I should keep my mouth shut and listen to the others. But knowing a little about Communist tactics from my dealings with the FBI, I suggested that we propose a resolution to the executive committee with language that we knew a Communist couldn't accept and have Olivia submit it in the next meeting the following week and see what happened.

"We wrote out what was essentially an innocuous declaration of principles ending with a phrase in which HICCASP's executive board reaffirmed its "belief in free enterprise and the Democratic system and repudiates Communism as desirable for the United States." The next week, we got together while Olivia attended the executive committee meeting. After an hour or so, the phone rang. It was Olivia. "They voted it down," she said. She joined us later and said she'd been the only one in favor of our resolution. It was all the proof we needed: HICCASP had become a Communist front organization hiding behind a few well-intentioned Hollywood celebrities to give it credibility. The next day, the twelve of us resigned, not only from the board, but the entire organization. We were the last front of respectability for HICCASP and within a week it was out of business - but not the people running it. They erased the name of HICCASP from the office door but put up the title of a new group - it was the same people with the same objectives behind a new front group.

"The strike and the efforts to gain control over HICCASP and other organizations had a profound effect on me. More than anything else, it was the Communists' attempted takeover of Hollywood and its worldwide weekly audience of more than five hundred million people that led me to accept a nomination to serve as president of the Screen Actors Guild and, indirectly at least, set me on the road that would lead me into politics. One of the best reviews I ever got didn't involve a movie but came from a fellow actor testifying in court. Sterling Hayden, who'd been among those flirting with Communism before later renouncing it, said: "Ronald Reagan was a one-man battalion of opposition" to the attempted Communist takeover of Hollywood during the 1946 strike. Now I knew from firsthand experience how Communists used lies, deceit, violence, or any other tactic that suited them to advance the cause of Soviet expansionism. I knew from the experience of hand-to-hand combat that America faced no more insidious or evil threat than that of Communism.

"During the late 1940s, one side effect of the attempted Communist infiltration of our industry was a kind of national backlash against Hollywood. As president of the Screen Actors Guild, I began speaking out to defend the industry. By now, I guess I was beginning to undergo a political transformation. As I've said, I'd emerged from the war a liberal. I think my political transformation began with my exposure to the business-as-usual attitude of many civil service bureaucrats during the war; then came the attempted Communist take-over of the picture business, which a lot of my liberal friends refused to admit ever happened; next, I had a brief experience living in a country that promised the kind of womb-to-tomb utopian benevolence a lot of these liberal friends wanted to bring to America. In 1949, I spent four months in England filming *The Hasty Heart* while the Labor Party was in power. I saw firsthand how the welfare state sapped incentive to work from many people in a wonderful and dynamic country.

"Probably because of my dad's influence and my experiences during the Depression, I had loved the Democratic Party. I agreed with Thomas Jefferson, its founder, who said: "Democrats consider the people as the safest depository of power in the last resort; they cherish them, therefore, and wish to leave in them all the powers to the exercise of which they are competent - the equal rights of every man and the happiness of every individual are now acknowledged to be the only legitimate objects of government." But the party had begun to change drastically in the thirties. Jefferson repeatedly said that the best government was the *smallest* government that "governments are not the masters of the people, but the servants of the people governed." Abe Lincoln once said, "The principles of Jefferson are the definitions and the axioms of a free society." But during the Depression, the Democrats began to repudiate many of these principles while creating a government that grew ever larger and increasingly demanded the right to regulate and plan the social and economic life of the country and move into arenas best left to private enterprise.

"Our federal bureaucracy expanded relentlessly during the post-war years and, almost always with the best of intentions, it began leading America along the path to a silent form of socialism. Our government wasn't nationalizing the railroads or the banks, but it was confiscating a disproportionate share of the nation's wealth through excessive taxes, and indirectly seizing control of the day-to-day management of our businesses with rules and regulations that often gave Washington bureaucrats the power of life and death over them. Well, pretty soon my speeches in defense of Hollywood were beginning to take on a new tone. And I received a telephone call that was to change my life and enrich it forever after.

"The telephone call was from director Mervyn LeRoy, who told me an actress working on one of his pictures needed my help. The young woman, Nancy Davis, was extremely upset because the name of another actress identified as Nancy Davis had appeared on the membership rosters of several Communist front groups and she was receiving notices of their meetings in her mail. As president of the Screen Actors Guild, I did a little research and found out that there was more than one Nancy Davis connected with show business - in fact there were several - and it took me only a few minutes to establish that Mervyn's Nancy Davis was not the one who belonged to several Communist front groups. Mervyn called back and said his assurances hadn't been enough to satisfy the young lady. "She's a worrier," he said. "She's still worried that people are going to think she's a Communist. Why don't you give her a call? I think she will take it better from you than from me. Just take her out to dinner and tell her the whole story yourself."

"I took her to a restaurant on the Sunset Strip and soon realized that Mervyn hadn't been exaggerating when he'd said she was really steamed up over having been confused with someone else. Pretty soon, we weren't talking any more about her problem, but about her mother, who had been a Broadway actress, and her father, a prominent surgeon, and our lives in general. Although we'd agreed to call it an early night, I didn't want the evening to end, so I said: "Have you ever seen Sophie Tucker?" She's singing at Ciro's just down the street. Why don't we go see the first show?" Well, she'd never heard Sophie Tucker before so we went to Ciro's to catch the first show. Then we stayed for the second show and we got home about three o'clock in the morning. I invited her to dinner the following night and we went to the Malibu Inn.

"After that, we dated occasionally, but both of us continued to date other people, and now and then our paths would cross while we were out with someone else. This had been going on for several months when I found myself booked for a speech to the Junior League Convention at the Del Coronado Hotel in San Diego. I wanted to share the ride with someone and wondered whom I should ask to join me. Then it suddenly occurred to me there was really only one person I wanted to share it with - Nancy Davis. I called her and she accepted and said she was a member of the Junior League in Chicago. Pretty soon, Nancy was the only one I was calling for dates. And one night over dinner as we sat at a table for two, I said, "Let's get married."

"She deserved a more romantic proposal than that, but - bless her - she put her hand on mine, looked into my eyes, and said, "Let's." I have spent many hours of my life giving speeches and expressing my opinions. But it is almost impossible for me to express fully how deeply I love Nancy and how much she has filled my life. From the start, our marriage was like an adolescent's dream of what a marriage should be. It was rich and full from the beginning, and it has gotten more so with each passing day. Nancy moved into my heart and replaced an emptiness that I'd been trying to ignore for a long time. Coming home to her is like coming out of the cold into a warm, fire lit room. I miss her if she just steps out of the room.

"Although I was pleased with several of the pictures that I made as a free lance, there were two or three that I wish I hadn't said yes to - and after a while I began worrying a little about the direction my career and Hollywood in general were taking. After Nancy and I talked it over, I decided to begin turning down roles in bad pictures and holding out until something really good came along. Our first child, Patricia Ann, had been born, and she had added lots of joy to the Reagan household. But financially, they were pretty lean and sometimes difficult times. In 1954, the General Electric Company was in the market for a new television program, and proposed a weekly dramatic anthology in which I would only act several times a season but serve as the host every week.

"I liked the idea because it offered me a chance to share in the growing financial prosperity of television while avoiding the kind of typecasting that acting in the same role week after week in a regular series brought with it. My new job called upon me to play a supporting role in an extraordinary experiment by American industry. Until then, most of America's industrial giants had tended to function under a strong central management within a single geographic region - United States Steel in Pittsburgh and General Motors in Detroit, for instance. But Ralph Cordiner, General Electric's chairman, a remarkable and foresighted businessman, believed GE would grow more dynamically if he dispersed its manufacturing operations around the country. Smaller divisions headed by strong local managers who had considerable autonomy over their products and manufacturing operations, he thought, ought to be more competitive and more responsive to the marketplace than a large, unwieldy organization dominated by a powerful head office, and I think he was right.

"Cordiner implemented his vision on a grand scale, establishing 139 GE plants in thirty-nine states. As an adjunct to my job on the television show, he asked me to travel to GE plants around the country as a kind of goodwill ambassador from the home office. Sending the host of the GE Theater to the far-flung plants, he thought, would demonstrate that the New York office cared about company employees no matter where they were and would also help forge a closer link between the plants and the communities where they were located. Local managers were instructed to take me to local events. About a year or two after the tours began, the GE representative who always accompanied me told me I was scheduled to speak to a group of company employees who had been working on a local charity fund-raising project. I think everybody expected me to get up and tell a few Hollywood stories as usual and then sit down. But instead, I decided to give a speech about the pride of giving and the importance of doing things without waiting for the government to do it for you. I pointed out that when individuals or private groups were involved in helping the needy, none of the contributions were spent on overhead or administrative costs, unlike government relief programs where $2 was often spent on overhead for every $1 that went to needy people. When I sat down, my remarks got a huge ovation.

"Well, that changed everything. From then on, whenever I went to a GE plant, in addition to meeting workers, they'd schedule a speech or two for me to a local organization like the United Fund or Chamber of Commerce; before long, the company began to get requests for me to speak before larger audiences - state conventions of service organizations and groups like the Executives Club in Chicago and the Commonwealth Club in San Francisco. Initially, my speeches were only about the picture business, but after a while I began trying to make them a kind of warning to others. This is what had happened in Hollywood; it they weren't careful, people in other occupations might soon find themselves in the same fix as those of us in Hollywood and be denied fair treatment by the government. Those GE tours became almost a postgraduate course in political science for me. I was seeing how government really operated and affected people in America, not how it was taught in school.

"From hundreds of people in every part of the country, I heard complaints about how the ever-expanding federal government was encroaching on liberties we'd always taken for granted. As time went on, the portion of my speech about government began to grow longer and I began to shorten the Hollywood part. Pretty soon, it became basically a warning to people about the threat of government. Finally, the Hollywood part just got lost and I was out there beating the bushes for private enterprise. No government has ever voluntarily reduced itself in size - and that, in a way, became my theme. In 1958, our second child, Ron, was born, bringing more joy into our lives. In 1960, after leading the Screen Actors Guild in its first major strike in history in my fifth term as president, I resigned after becoming a partner in a production company, and therefore, from the union's point of view, I was no longer a working stiff but a producer.

"In Hollywood, I'd found more than I'd ever expected life to give me. For many, many reasons, these were very happy years for Nancy and me." (Courtesy of Simon and Schuster)

———

John F. Kennedy

American Spirit

November 18, 1961

In recent months I have spoken many times about how difficult and dangerous a period it is through which we now move. I would like to take this opportunity to say a word about the American spirit in this time of trial.

In the most critical periods of our nation's history, there have always been those fringes of our society who have sought to escape their own responsibility by finding a simple solution, an appealing slogan, or a convenient scapegoat. Financial crises could be explained by the presence of too many immigrants or too few greenbacks.

War could be attributed to munitions makers or international bankers. Peace conferences failed because we were duped by the British or tricked by the French or deceived by the Russians.

It was not the presence of Soviet troops in Eastern Europe that drove it to Communism; it was the sell-out at Yalta. It was not a civil war that removed China from the free world; it was treason in high places. At times these fanatics have achieved a temporary success among those who lack the will or the vision to face unpleasant tasks or unsolved problems.

But in time the basic good sense and stability of the great American consensus has always prevailed.

Now we are face to face once again with a period of heightened peril. The risks are great, the burdens heavy, and the problems incapable of swift or lasting solution. And under the strains and frustrations imposed by constant tension and harassment, the discordant voices of extremism are heard once again in the land. Men who are unwilling to face up to the danger from without are convinced that the real danger comes from within.

They look suspiciously at their neighbors and their leaders. They call for a 'man on horseback' because they do not trust the people. They find treason in our finest churches, in our highest court, and even in the treatment of our water. They equate the Democratic Party with the welfare state, the welfare state with socialism, and socialism with communism. They object quite rightly to politics' intruding on the military — but they are anxious for the military to engage in politics.

But you and I and most Americans take a different view of our peril. We know that it comes from without, not within. It must be met by quiet preparedness, not provocative speeches.

And the steps taken this year to bolster our defenses—to increase our missile forces, to put more planes on alert, to provide more airlift and sealift and ready divisions—to make more certain than ever before that this nation has all the power it will need to deter any attack of any kind—those steps constitute the most effective answer that can be made to those who would sow the seeds of doubt and hate.

So let us not heed these counsels of fear and suspicion. Let us concentrate more on keeping enemy bombers and missiles away from our shores, and concentrate less on keeping neighbors away from our shelters. Let us devote more energy to organize the free and friendly nations of the world, with common trade and strategic goals, and devote less energy to organizing armed bands of civilian guerrillas that are more likely to supply local vigilantes than national vigilance.

Let our patriotism be reflected in the creation of confidence rather than crusades of suspicion. Let us prove we think our country great by striving to make it greater. And, above all, let us remember that, however serious the outlook, the one great irreversible trend in world history is on the side of liberty—and so, for all time to come, are we.

———

The Preservation of Civilization: address delivered at the autumn convocation of the University of Toronto, October 27, 1950, The Right Honorable Louis Stephen St. Laurent

It is a melancholy reflection on the times we live in that we should feel obliged to be concerned over the preservation of civilization. Half a century ago, when I was an undergraduate at another university, I doubt if any of us gave a thought to this question. In those days we were nearly all confident that civilization was advancing steadily over the face of the globe, that the only serious obstacles to the advance of civilization were ignorance and barbarism, and that these obstacles would eventually be overcome.

At the beginning of this century very few people dreamed that a menace to the existence of civilization might arise in the very heart of the civilized world. Yet that is precisely what has happened in the twentieth century with Fascism. Nazism and Communism alike.

What is more, the enslavement of the minds of human beings is not an incidental feature of totalitarianism, whether it takes the form of Fascism or Nazism or Communism. The very essence of the totalitarian state is the regimentation of all aspects of human life and all forms of human expression. I am sure all of us are convinced if the human mind is enslaved, civilization will eventually disappear. I think most of us would also agree that, given time, any totalitarian structure would be bound to collapse because no organized society can hope to endure indefinitely without some means of training independent and truly educated minds. But the process of internal decay and collapse might easily require several generations, during which the totalitarian state by its very nature would remain a threat to the existence of all its free neighbours. In the case of a totalitarian state with the population and resources of the Soviet Union, such a threat is, in fact, a menace to civilization itself.

I say a totalitarian state, by its very nature, must remain a threat to its free neighbours. I believe this proposition is incontrovertible. The totalitarian state can be maintained only by armed force. That armed force may exist primarily to keep the subject population in slavery but its very existence constitutes a threat to other nations without equal strength. And this menace is redoubled because the masters of such a state justify the maintenance of armed might on the ground that their own state is really the one which is in danger and must dominate all its neighbours for its own preservation.

The Nazi state was founded on the doctrine that the German people were a master race with a right, as such, to conquer and rule the lesser breeds of the human family. Nazi rule was based openly and nakedly on force, and ten years ago virtually the whole world was convinced that unless this force was destroyed it would destroy everything worthwhile in the world.

The terrible menace of Nazi domination — and we should never forget it was a terrible menace — was destroyed by a mighty effort on the part of the rest of the world. In overcoming the Nazi menace, the Russian people had a heroic part. I believe the vast majority of people all over the free world were ready, in 1945, to cooperate with the Russians in peace as they had cooperated with us in war.

We could hardly be blamed for hoping that the victory, won at so terrible a cost, would give real peace to the world and that it would give humanity a real chance to devote its energies to constructive activities. In 1945, many of us cherished the hope that. Even if full cooperation with the Soviet Union could not be achieved, we might at least reach a tolerable modus vivendi based upon a common weariness of war and a common desire for peace.

In 1945, many people felt that Communism, after all, was not the same thing as Nazism. Of course, the philosophical basis of Communism was repugnant to most of us and the barbarity of Communist practices was even more repugnant, but, at least, the Communists did not claim to be a master race with a natural right to dominate the whole world by force. The Nazi state glorified war; the Communist state had never openly done so. The goal of Communism was said to be the material welfare of mankind and, in the Communist ideology, force was looked upon as a means to an end, not the end itself.

It is precisely this theoretical goal of increased material welfare for the less fortunate part of humanity, accompanied by the Communist propaganda in favour of racial equality, which has constituted at once the main appeal and the greatest ideological danger of totalitarian Communism. The fact that Communism, in its Soviet form, denies the essential importance of the human being and the possibility of the individual ever influencing his own fate, in this world or in the hereafter, is often lost sight of by those to whom the Communist myth appeals.

On the other hand, this appeal of Communism to the unfortunate and the oppressed has had one good effect. It has sharpened our realization that we must do something ourselves to remove the social evils which provide the breeding ground for Communist support.

Mr. Arnold Toynbee has pointed out in a recent article that, if the Communists continue in their present course, "we may see them rouse the Western World to cure itself of the faults for which the Communists denounce it, and to fulfill, in our own Western way, any admirable aims that are on Communism's official agenda."

Of course it is not the intention of the Communists to push our Western civilization into putting its house in better order, but there are increasing grounds for believing that is what they may be accomplishing.

The so-called "iron curtain" has failed to conceal from the Western world the wide disparity between the theoretical aims of Communism and the actual social accomplishments of Communist totalitarianism, and the number of those in the Western World who are deceived by Soviet propaganda diminishes week by week. But the military strength of Communist Russia and the policies of its masters in these postwar years have convinced all but the blindest among us that the only hope of immediate security for the rest of the world lies in building up armed strength sufficient to be an effective deterrent to the potential aggression of this latest military tyranny.

Moreover, I think we all recognize, after the terrible experiences of this twentieth century, that a third world war, no matter how complete our ultimate victory, could not fail to be a major disaster for civilization. If war should come between those who profess the gross materialism of Communist ideology and those who accept the moral ideals of our Christian civilization, I am firmly convinced that the powers of evil, like the gates of Hell, would not prevail. But such a struggle, regardless of the outcome, would itself be a disaster. Consequently all of us who are seriously concerned about the preservation of civilization simply have no choice but to do our part in providing the absolutely indispensable insurance against that disaster. Our first duty to civilization is, therefore, the provision of sufficient military strength, including the industrial strength on which real military strength today is based, to make the risk of starting another war a risk not worth taking.

For the last two years, the building up of that deterrent strength through the North Atlantic Alliance and, more recently, through the United Nations action in Korea, has been the first preoccupation of the Government of Canada and of the governments of the free nations with which we are associated. The provision of effective insurance against another world war is likely to continue to be one of our main problems for a good many years to come.

This policy of insurance through strength, in these times of rapid technological advance, is bound to make tremendous demands upon our universities to provide scientific and professional training and also the higher kinds of technical training. These demands are particularly severe in a country like ours, which is developing new resources at such an amazing rate, and it is very important that all these demands should be met, and met adequately. In meeting them, the universities are performing essential, national services.

But we have to recognize at the same time that there is another side to the preservation of civilization. It will never be enough to have sufficient strength to deter or restrain the external enemies of civilization. The task of keeping alive and flourishing, the civilization we are organizing ourselves to protect may not be quite so urgent in the short run, but it is equally vital if we are thinking not in terms of one or two years but of one or two decades.

A free civilization cannot be preserved behind an iron curtain, however strong. And I doubt if anyone believes that there can be any enduring civilization without freedom for individual men and women.

While I was preparing my notes to this address I came across a lecture by Professor Jacques Maritain, whom I understand is well known in this University. The lecture originally delivered in Paris in 1939 was published in an English version in 1942 and is entitled "The Twilight of Civilization".

In the original lecture Professor Maritain said, "each time that someone in any country cedes to some infiltration or the totalitarian spirit, under any form whatsoever, under any disguise, one battle for civilization has been lost".

Then in the foreword written in 1942, he used these words: "The defeat or Germany will not solve all the problems of freedom to be won, of civilization to be rescued and rebuilt. But it is a necessary condition if they are to be solved and the world freed from the slavery which today threatens each and everyone or us."

What all this means is that we have only begun the task of preserving civilization when we have provided security against the forces of barbarism from without. We must also provide security against the influences of barbarism we have found in the midst of our civilized communities. To preserve civilization, we have to nourish the spirit within.

Our Western world has accepted the doctrine that men and women have the right to choose — and to dismiss — their governments for themselves; and to order their affairs as they see fit. It is evident, therefore, that if we are to preserve civilization, we must keep alive in our populations an attachment to the values of civilization; and we must make sure that the benefits of civilization are available to the many and not reserved for the few.

We cannot neglect the less fortunate in our own midst, nor can we ignore the plight or nations less fortunate than our own. The preservation or civilization requires us to help those untold millions, most of them in Asia, to improve their standards of life and to achieve a situation they will feel it is worthwhile to defend. Despite our relatively small population, we have advantages here in Canada which fit us to contribute effectively to a combined effort to convince the less fortunate peoples that even on the material plane the free world has more to offer than Communism. It is not without significance that Canada should have furnished the first Director for the Technical Assistance Programme of the United Nations.

In addition to the material benefits there must however, be a fount of spiritual values in our free societies. We in the Western world have adopted the conception of good and evil from the Hebrew and Greek civilizations. This concept has been transformed and transmitted to us through our Christian traditions. It comprises a belief in the intrinsic value of every individual human being and a sense of obligation to our neighbour. Its very essence is freedom. And the nurture of this spirit of our free society is the primary function of the universities. It is even more important than the obligations to train men and women for scientific and professional pursuits.

The Universities are, without question, among the most precious of our national institutions. Now I recognize, and I believe most Canadians recognize, the wisdom of the provision of our constitution, which made education perhaps the most important of all those subjects, entrusted to the provincial authorities. This provision was designed primarily to safeguard both of the two cultural traditions which we Canadians possess and which, year by year, we are coming to cherish more and more, as we realize how greatly they enrich our national life. The entrusting of education to the provincial authorities has the further advantage of providing a measure of insurance against too great a degree of uniformity in our educational systems. No one with any real respect for our history and tradition would wish to disturb that constitutional position. At the same time, I think many of us recognize increasingly that some means must be found to ensure to our universities the financial capacity to perform the many services, which are required in the interest of the whole nation. I hope you, Mr. Chancellor, in association with your colleagues in another of your capacities, will be able to help us to find a proper solution of that difficult problem.

In seeking a solution of the problem we must never lose sight of the fact that essential though it is to provide for the training of scientists and of men and women for the professions, this is not the highest national service the universities perform. Their highest service is to educate men and women in that liberal and humane tradition which is the glory of our Christian civilization. The first task of a true University is to keep alive the flame of civilization itself. This great academic community, this great federation of Universities with their rich and varied traditions, here in Toronto, has been faithful to that essential trust. And that is the reason I shall be proud, from today, to number myself among the alumni of the University of Toronto.

(Source: St-Laurent, Louis. *The preservation of civilization.* Ottawa: Information Division, Dept. of External Affairs, 1950. 5 p.)

———

THURSDAY, JANUARY 20, 1949

A former county judge, Senator and Vice President, Harry S. Truman had taken the oath of office first on April 12, 1945, upon the death of President Roosevelt. The President went to the East Portico of the Capitol to take the oath of office on two Bibles—the personal one he had used for the first oath, and a Gutenberg Bible donated by the citizens of Independence, Missouri.

Mr. Vice President, Mr. Chief Justice, and fellow citizens, I accept with humility the honor, which the American people have conferred upon me. I accept it with a deep resolve to do all that I can for the welfare of this Nation and for the peace of the world.

In performing the duties of my office, I need the help and prayers of every one of you. I ask for your encouragement and your support. The tasks we face are difficult, and we can accomplish them only if we work together.

Each period of our national history has had its special challenges. Those that confront us now are as momentous as any in the past. Today marks the beginning not only of a new administration, but also of a period that will be eventful, perhaps decisive, for us and for the world.

It may be our lot to experience, and in large measure to bring about, a major turning point in the long history of the human race. The first half of this century has been marked by unprecedented and brutal attacks on the rights of man, and by the two most frightful wars in history. The supreme need of our time is for men to learn to live together in peace and harmony.

The peoples of the earth face the future with grave uncertainty, composed almost equally of great hopes and great fears. In this time of doubt, they look to the United States as never before for good will, strength, and wise leadership.

It is fitting, therefore, that we take this occasion to proclaim to the world the essential principles of the faith by which we live, and to declare our aims to all peoples.

The American people stand firm in the faith, which has inspired this Nation from the beginning. We believe that all men have a right to equal justice under law and equal opportunity to share in the common good. We believe that all men have the right to freedom of thought and expression. We believe that all men are created equal because they are created in the image of God.

From this faith we will not be moved.

The American people desire, and are determined to work for, a world in which all nations and all peoples are free to govern themselves as they see fit, and to achieve a decent and satisfying life. Above all else, our people desire, and are determined to work for, peace on earth—a just and lasting peace—based on genuine agreement freely arrived at by equals.

In the pursuit of these aims, the United States and other like- minded nations find themselves directly opposed by a regime with contrary aims and a totally different concept of life.

That regime adheres to a false philosophy, which purports to offer freedom, security, and greater opportunity to mankind. Misled by this philosophy, many peoples have sacrificed their liberties only to learn to their sorrow that deceit and mockery, poverty and tyranny, are their reward.

That false philosophy is Communism.

Communism is based on the belief that man is so weak and inadequate that he is unable to govern himself, and therefore requires the rule of strong masters.

R.E. "Gus" Payne

Democracy is based on the conviction that man has the moral and intellectual capacity, as well as the inalienable right, to govern himself with reason and justice.

Communism subjects the individual to arrest without lawful cause, punishment without trial, and forced labor as the chattel of the state. It decrees what information he shall receive, what art he shall produce, what leaders he shall follow, and what thoughts he shall think.

Democracy maintains that government is established for the benefit of the individual, and is charged with the responsibility of protecting the rights of the individual and his freedom in the exercise of his abilities.

Communism maintains that social wrongs can be corrected only by violence.

Democracy has proved that social justice can be achieved through peaceful change.

Communism holds that the world is so deeply divided into opposing classes that war is inevitable.

Democracy holds that free nations can settle differences justly and maintain lasting peace.

These differences between communism and democracy do not concern the United States alone. People everywhere are coming to realize that what is involved is material well being, human dignity, and the right to believe in and worship God.

I state these differences, not to draw issues of belief as such, but because the actions resulting from the Communist philosophy are a threat to the efforts of free nations to bring about world recovery and lasting peace.

Since the end of hostilities, the United States has invested its substance and its energy in a great constructive effort to restore peace, stability, and freedom to the world.

We have sought no territory and we have imposed our will on none. We have asked for no privileges we would not extend to others.

We have constantly and vigorously supported the United Nations and related agencies as a means of applying democratic principles to international relations. We have consistently advocated and relied upon peaceful settlement of disputes among nations.

We have made every effort to secure agreement on effective international control of our most powerful weapon, and we have worked steadily for the limitation and control of all armaments.

We have encouraged, by precept and example, the expansion of world trade on a sound and fair basis.

Almost a year ago, in company with 16 free nations of Europe, we launched the greatest cooperative economic program in history. The purpose of that unprecedented effort is to invigorate and strengthen democracy in Europe, so that the free people of that continent can resume their rightful place in the forefront of civilization and can contribute once more to the security and welfare of the world.

Our efforts have brought new hope to all mankind. We have beaten back despair and defeatism. We have saved a number of countries from losing their liberty. Hundreds of millions of people all over the world now agree with us, that we need not have war—that we can have peace.

The initiative is ours.

We are moving on with other nations to build an even stronger structure of international order and justice. We shall have as our partners countries which, no longer solely concerned with the problem of national survival, are now working to improve the standards of living of all their people. We are ready to undertake new projects to strengthen the free world.

In the coming years, our program for peace and freedom will emphasize four major courses of action. First, we will continue to give unfaltering support to the United Nations and related agencies, and we will continue to search for ways to strengthen their authority and increase their effectiveness. We believe that the United Nations will be strengthened by the new nations, which are being formed in lands now advancing toward self-government under democratic principles.

Second, we will continue our programs for world economic recovery.

This means, first of all, that we must keep our full weight behind the European recovery program. We are confident of the success of this major venture in world recovery. We believe that our partners in this effort will achieve the status of self-supporting nations once again.

In addition, we must carry out our plans for reducing the barriers to world trade and increasing its volume. Economic recovery and peace itself depend on increased world trade.

Third, we will strengthen freedom-loving nations against the dangers of aggression.

We are now working out with a number of countries a joint agreement designed to strengthen the security of the North Atlantic area. Such an agreement would take the form of a collective defense arrangement within the terms of the United Nations Charter.

We have already established such a defense pact for the Western Hemisphere by the treaty of Rio de Janeiro.

The primary purpose of these agreements is to provide unmistakable proof of the joint determination of the free countries to resist armed attack from any quarter. Each country participating in these arrangements must contribute all it can to the common defense.

If we can make it sufficiently clear, in advance, that any armed attack affecting our national security would be met with overwhelming force, the armed attack might never occur.

I hope soon to send to the Senate a treaty respecting the North Atlantic security plan.

In addition, we will provide military advice and equipment to free nations, which will cooperate with us in the maintenance of peace and security.

Fourth, we must embark on a bold new program for making the benefits of our scientific advances and industrial progress available for the improvement and growth of underdeveloped areas.

More than half the people of the world are living in conditions approaching misery. Their food is inadequate. They are victims of disease. Their economic life is primitive and stagnant. Their poverty is a handicap and a threat both to them and to more prosperous areas.

For the first time in history, humanity possesses the knowledge and the skill to relieve the suffering of these people.

The United States is pre-eminent among nations in the development of industrial and scientific techniques. The material resources which we can afford to use for the assistance of other peoples are limited. But our imponderable resources in technical knowledge are constantly growing and are inexhaustible.

I believe that we should make available to peace-loving peoples the benefits of our store of technical knowledge in order to help them realize their aspirations for a better life. And, in cooperation with other nations, we should foster capital investment in areas needing development.

Our aim should be to help the free peoples of the world, through their own efforts, to produce more food, more clothing, and more materials for housing, and more mechanical power to lighten their burdens.

We invite other countries to pool their technological resources in this undertaking. Their contributions will be warmly welcomed. This should be a cooperative enterprise in which all nations work together through the United Nations and its specialized agencies wherever practicable. It must be a worldwide effort for the achievement of peace, plenty, and freedom.

With the cooperation of business, private capital, agriculture, and labor in this country, this program can greatly increase the industrial activity in other nations and can raise substantially their standards of living.

Such new economic developments must be devised and controlled to benefit the peoples of the areas in which they are established. Guarantees to the investor must be balanced by guarantees in the interest of the people whose resources and whose labor go into these developments.

The old imperialism—exploitation for foreign profit—has no place in our plans. What we envisage is a program of development based on the concepts of democratic fair dealing.

All countries, including our own, will greatly benefit from a constructive program for the better use of the world's human and natural resources. Experience shows that our commerce with other countries expands as they progress industrially and economically.

Greater production is the key to prosperity and peace. And the key to greater production is a wider and more vigorous application of modern scientific and technical knowledge.

Only by helping the least fortunate of its members to help themselves can the human family achieve the decent, satisfying life that is the right of all people.

Democracy alone can supply the vitalizing force to stir the peoples of the world into triumphant action, not only against their human oppressors, but also against their ancient enemies— hunger, misery, and despair.

On the basis of these four major courses of action we hope to help create the conditions that will lead eventually to personal freedom and happiness for all mankind.

If we are to be successful in carrying out these policies, it is clear that we must have continued prosperity in this country and we must keep ourselves strong.

Slowly but surely we are weaving a world fabric of international security and growing prosperity.

We are aided by all who wish to live in freedom from fear—even by those who live today in fear under their own governments.

We are aided by all who want relief from the lies of propaganda— who desire truth and sincerity.

We are aided by all who desire self-government and a voice in deciding their own affairs.

We are aided by all who long for economic security—for the security and abundance that men in free societies can enjoy.

We are aided by all who desire freedom of speech, freedom of religion, and freedom to live their own lives for useful ends.

Our allies are the millions who hunger and thirst after righteousness.

In due time, as our stability becomes manifest, as more and more nations come to know the benefits of democracy and to participate in growing abundance, I believe that those countries which now oppose us will abandon their delusions and join with the free nations of the world in a just settlement of international differences.

Events have brought our American democracy to new influence and new responsibilities. They will test our courage, our devotion to duty, and our concept of liberty.

But I say to all men, what we have achieved in liberty, we will surpass in greater liberty.

Steadfast in our faith in the Almighty, we will advance toward a world where man's freedom is secure.

To that end we will devote our strength, our resources, and our firmness of resolve. With God's help, the future of mankind will be assured in a world of justice, harmony, and peace."

Random recollection of other thoughts...

The New York Herald Tribune, August 19. 1955:

"The House Committee on Un-American Activities yesterday ended a four-day hearing here at which only one of twenty-three show business witnesses cooperated in spotlighting Communist infiltration of the entertainment world...During the hearings eighteen witnesses invoked the protection of the 5th Amendment when asked about Communist activities in the theater, radio and television and in unions of entertainers. Four others defied the committee on other grounds and face contempt of Congress charges."

_____

America is like a healthy body and its resistance is threefold: its patriotism, its morality, and its spiritual life. If we can undermine these three areas, America will collapse from within. (Joseph Stalin)

_____

How do you tell a communist? Well, it's someone who reads Marx and Lenin. And how do you tell an anti-communist? It's someone who understands Marx and Lenin. (Remarks in Arlington, Virginia September 25, 1987)

_____

"The communists have lost the cold war, but the west has not yet won it." (Richard Nixon)

_____

In the end we beat them with Levi 501 jeans. Seventy-two years of communist indoctrination and propaganda was drowned out by a three-ounce Sony Walkman. A huge totalitarian system has been brought to its knees because nobody wants to wear Bulgarian shoes. Now they're lunch, and we're number one on the planet. (PJ O'Rourke)

R.E. "Gus" Payne

———

The only program the FBI was not able to put in motion was its plan for emergency detention in case of national emergency. Nevertheless, the bureau prepared for this eventuality throughout the cold-war decade. The bureau, often without the full knowledge of the Justice Department and under standards far broader than those laid down by Congress in 1950, maintained a number of detention lists. The Security Index had top priority in case of national crisis. This list, which included the communist leaders, had 11,982 names. Next in line for preventive detention were members of the party, a list of 17,783 persons contained in the bureau's Communist Index. These were only the names in FBI headquarters files. FBI field offices listed over 200,000 persons considered by the FBI to constitute a danger to national security in time of crisis. (The crimes of the U.S. Inteligence Agencies by Morton Halperin, Jerry Beman, Robert Borosage, Christine Marwick, 1976)

EPILOGUE

With the Soviet Union no longer in existence, the world's countries are turning their attention to the last major communist nation that has influence. China will have to tread lightly, especially with the return of Hong Kong, a valuable port that was the refuge for millions of democratic citizens. China has promised a "one country, two systems" policy, but that is only drawing more criticism. Communism can no longer grow, it can only mature. However, the maturing process is turning it into more of a capitalist country. If Beijing wants to be welcomed into the community of nations with the stature its size and wealth ought to command, China will have to convince the West that it is ready and able to live by the world's new rules.

It was on October 1, 1949 that Mao Tsetung pronounced the establishment of the new Chinese Communist state: the People's Republic of China. It was for this reason that Mao and over 10,000 people set off on what was to be called The Long March. They began in the Jiangxi province where their ranks rapidly grew and became known as the Fourth Red Army. It was comprised of peasants and soldiers who were in favor of a communist regime, or were in opposition to Chiang Kai-shek's Nationalist views. Mao's army never numbered more that 85,000 peasants, while Chiang's forces, the Kuomintang, numbered 200,000 well-equipped troops. The odds were definitely against Mao. It was for this reason that he favored guerrilla warfare. Mao described these tactics in his Little Red Book:

When the enemy advances, we retreat.

When he camps, we harass.

When he tires, we attack.

When he retires, we pursue.

Our weapons are supplied us by the enemy.

I do not believe socialist ideas will ever prevail in the United States but would I have believed this in the 1940s or in 1950 when Matt Cvetic appeared at his first hearing? People in the United States have different cultures, religions, and beliefs that would bring down anyone trying to make all the people happy. No matter how hard we try, we cannot make everyone equal, except, perhaps, under the law.

If you look at United States today, it has a democracy that works. The government is a contributing factor to why United States is considered a Super Power. The Cold War on the ground is over and the apocalyptic threat of a civilization-destroying nuclear world war has receded. The Soviet Union is no more, and communists and communism, although not gone, are going. Communism and the Cold War, however, are far from over. This past century has seen war, revolution, mass murder, human butchery, terror, and cruelty on an extraordinary scale. Considering what we know of the history of the human race, we can expect this to continue.

What we tried to do here, in this book, is give Matt Cvetic some credit for his courage and a little admiration for his love of country. He was not a perfect man but for an incredibly long nine years he did what many others could not do. While it may be true that he was a womanizer and that he drank too much, it is also true that this did not prevent him from doing a very daring job that those purer in mind and soul would not have attempted.

Matt Cvetic should be remembered for what he did for his country.

R.E. "Gus" Payne

BIBLIOGRAPHY

Agreement, August 9, 1950, *I Was a Communist for the FBI (Ziv Papers)*

Agreement Between Warner Brothers and Frederic W. Ziv Company, December 3, 1951

Robert Kenneth Carr, *The House Committee on Un-American Activities, 1945-1950* (Ithaca, N.Y.: Cornell University Press, 1952)

Alistair Cooke, *A Generation on Trial: U.S.A. vs. Alger Hiss* (New York: Knopf, 1950)

Cvetic, Matt (as told to Pete Martin), "I Posed as a Communist for the FBI," *Saturday Evening Post,* July 15, 1950

Cvetic, Matt,*The Big Decision* (Hollywood, Calif.: The Big Decision, 1959)

Demaris, Ovid, *The Director: An Oral Biography of J. Edgar Hoover* (New York: Harper's Magazine Press, 1975)

M. J. Heale, *American Anti-Communism* (Baltimore: Johns Hopkins Press, 1990)

Hearings Regarding Communist Infiltration, 81st Cong., 2nd session, December 20-22, 1950

HUAC, *Expose of the Communist Party of Western Pennsylvania Based upon the Testimony of Matthew Cvetic, Undercover Agent,* Hearings, 81st Cong., 2nd session (Washington, D.C., 1950)

HUAC, *Current Strategy and Tactics of Communists in the United States, Greater Pittsburgh Area,* 86th Cong., 1st session (Washington, D.C., 1959)

William W. Keller, *The Liberals and J. Edgar Hoover* (Princeton, N.J.: Princeton University Press, 1989)

Klehr, Harvey, John Earl Haynes, and F.I. Firsov, *The Secret World of American Communism* (New Haven, Conn.: Yale University Press, 1995

R.E. *"Gus" Payne*

McCarthy, Joseph Senator, *"Speech at Wheeling, West Virginia,* February 9, 1950

Steve Nelson, *The Thirteenth Juror-The Inside Story of my Trial* (New York: Masses and Mainstream, 1955)

Kenneth O'Reilly, *Hoover and the Un-Americans: The FBI, HUAC, and the Red Menace (*Philadelphia: Temple University Press, 1983)

Philbrick, *I Led Three Lives* (New York: McGraw Hill Book Co., 1952)

Powers, Richard Gid, *Not Without Honor: The History of American Anticommunism* (New Haven: Yale University Press, 1998)

Reeves, Thomas C. *The Life and Times of Joe McCarthy* (New York: Stein and Day, 1982.

Selcraig, James Truett, *The Red Scare in the Midwest*, 1945-1955 (Ann Arbor, Mich: UMI Research Press, 1982

Seldes, George, *Witch Hunt: The Technique and Profit of Redbaiting* (New York:Random House, 1948)

U.S. Senate, Committee on the Judiciary, SISS, *Subversive Influence in Certain Industrial Plants: Eastern Pennsylvania,* Hearing, 83rd Cong., 2nd session (Washington, D.C., 1954)

Whitehead, Don, *The FBI Story,* (New York: Random House, 1956)

Newspapers

Pittsburgh Post-Gazette, February 21, 1950, p.1; April 15, 1953; October 13, 1968, Musmanno (Obituary)

Pittsburgh Press, April 3, 1949, p. 1F; February 19, 1950, p.1; February 20, 1950, p.2; February 24, 1950, p. 11; March 1, 31, 1950 (HUAC, Cvetic); March 2, 1950; March 6, 1950; March 15, 1950, p. 1; August 31, 1951; March 16, 1953; April 12, 1953;April 11, 1954; May 17, 1959; December 23, 1966, (Gunther obituary); October 15, 1968 (editorial); November 14, 1968 (editorial); February 9, 1978

Pittsburgh Sun-Telegraph, February 20, 1950, clipping; August 22, 1950; January 8, 1952

Variety, August 8, 1950

ABOUT THE AUTHOR

R. E. Payne is the author of "Caught in the Crossfire", published in 1994 and the subject of a NBC-TV movie starring Dennis Franz as Mr. Payne. He is, perhaps, best known for his investigative report, "The Death of Brandon Lee: The Untold Story". Published as a periodical, it is estimated to have sold over 300,000 copies.

Mr. Payne's "The End Of All Diseases", published 2003, is currently optioned as a major motion picture.

He is the director of two universities, the founder of the Foundation of Truth and Justice, Inc. and he serves as a member of numerous international educational organizations.

www.ingramcontent.com/pod-product-compliance
Lightning Source LLC
Chambersburg PA
CBHW020336290526
45785CB00005B/2039